iPhone Forensics

iPhone Forensics

Jonathan Zdziarski

O'REILLY®

Beijing · Cambridge · Farnham · Köln · Sebastopol · Taipei · Tokyo

iPhone Forensics

by Jonathan Zdziarski

Copyright © 2008 Jonathan Zdziarski. All rights reserved.
Printed in the United States of America.

Published by O'Reilly Media, Inc., 1005 Gravenstein Highway North, Sebastopol, CA 95472.

O'Reilly books may be purchased for educational, business, or sales promotional use. Online editions are also available for most titles (*http://safari.oreilly.com*). For more information, contact our corporate/institutional sales department: (800) 998-9938 or *corporate@oreilly.com*.

Editor: Andy Oram	**Indexer:** Fred Brown
Production Editor: Adam Witwer	**Cover Designer:** Karen Montgomery
Proofreader: Emily Quill	**Interior Designer:** David Futato
	Illustrator: Jessamyn Read

Printing History:

September 2008:   First Edition.

ISBN: 978-0-596-15358-8

[M]

1220018383

*To every device manufacturer
who, through lethargy and poor
hires, plays the lottery with our
personal information.*

Table of Contents

Foreword

The iPhone is a very useful tool, but you should be aware of some very important things. This book will shed some light about just how "private" a device like the iPhone really is.

The iPhone is essentially a full-fledged computer, running a slimmed down version of the Unix operating system and Apple's Leopard. Like most mainstream operating systems, deleting a file only deletes the reference to the data, and not the actual data. This is why data recovery programs work. For the iPhone, the same is also true, but in addition, the amount of data stored on the iPhone extends far beyond what is perceived to be stored on it or what is accessible through its user interface. This data is, however, accessible with the tools and procedures outlined in this book. A criminal might attempt to delete all of the data she thinks exists on the phone but, in most cases, will have only made it inaccessible to the average person. A criminal might also think simple security, such as a passcode, will safeguard self-incriminating evidence from the police. As you'll see, this too only keeps the average person out. Fortunately for you, if you are reading this book, you are not an average person.

My opinion on crime is this: any self-respecting criminal is likely to use a desktop computer with encryption or other tools to hide his dirty deeds. With strong encryption, new laws such as the Foreign Intelligence Surveillance Act—which gives the U.S. Government unfettered access to our private email, text messages, and voice conversations—can be rendered useless. Good encryption is effective, even against government bodies, but involves time and know-how. Fortunately, it's easy to catch a criminal with his pants down, unless he is very careful.

However, in my opinion, the list of criminals that can effectively use encryption, or other technical means of hiding their communication, is a very small list. Therefore, this book is going to help you catch most everyone else. With respect to the few who do outsmart the government, it can be more important to monitor endpoints of communication than the actual communication itself—that is, who is associated with who. Should a criminal's contacts be exposed, law enforcement officials can trace the date, time, and phone numbers back to actual people, easily cross-indexed with the massive databases our governments no doubt keeps. If a criminal is using an iPhone, she's already compromised her operation on some level.

Computer security is a never-ending war between those who desire to hide information and those who work to expose it. There's no telling who is winning, but this book can help tip the scales in favor of the good guys.

The detailed content of this book will appeal to various types of readers. Although it has its roots in police forensics (having been distributed to hundreds of law enforcement agencies prior to being published), this book will also prove very useful to computer security professionals and anyone seeking a deeper understanding of how the iPhone works.

It comes highly recommended to have this book in anyone's library.

—Cap'n Crunch

Preface

The iPhone has quickly become a market leader in mobile technology, finding its way into the corporate world and the everyday lives of millions of end users. The iPhone's wide range of functionality, combined with its mobile, "always on" design, has allowed it to be used as a functional mobile office. The cost of this productivity is the danger of storing sensitive data on the device. Any given iPhone is likely to contain sensitive information belonging to its owner, and some types of information that may belong to others—corporate email, documents, and photos, to name a few.

As the dark side of such a versatile device becomes more evident, so does a need to recover personal information from it.

Problem employees engage in activities that put the company at risk, sometimes leaving an evidence trail on corporately owned equipment. The use of digital forensics has become an effective tool in conducting investigations and evaluating what activities a suspect employee has engaged in. Recovering deleted email, voicemail, photos, and other digital evidence can expose an employee who is stealing from the company, having an affair at work, or committing other acts that a corporation may need to investigate.

Outside the corporate world, criminals have also adopted the iPhone. Over the past several months, much of the forensic information contained in this book has been used by over 200 different law enforcement agencies throughout the world to conduct electronic discovery and ultimately prosecute criminals. The evidence preserved by the iPhone has helped to locate, charge, and prosecute murderers, drug dealers, rapists, and even terrorists.

This book introduces the reader to digital forensics and outlines the technical procedures needed to recover low-level data from the iPhone—an otherwise closed device. The book is intended for lawful forensic examination of devices by corporate security officers, law enforcement personnel, and private forensic examiners. Some examples based on past cases involving crimes and corporate theft will be used to illustrate the process. Federal, state, and multinational agencies have helped to test and verify the procedures outlined in this book, and that information is now available for the private sector.

Many people take the iPhone's powerful design for granted and fail to understand the degree to which their sensitive information can be recovered. Because the iPhone is designed to provide for more than adequate storage needs, and because much of the content installed on the iPhone, such as music, remains static, the integrity of data can be preserved for long periods of time. As the device uses a solid-state flash memory, it is designed to minimize writes, and can preserve data even longer than a desktop computer might.

This book is designed to be a concise aid, and although a basic introduction to digital forensics is provided, it is by no means a complete course. Combining the information in this book with formal training in forensics and best practices in the field will help to ensure that evidence is correctly processed and admissible in a court of law.

Audience of This Book

This book is designed for corporate compliance and security personnel, law enforcement officers, and digital forensic examiners. The average geek and those casually wanting to look down the rabbit hole will also find a wealth of information in this book. If you've got some basic computer skills, this book will also come in handy for those one-off needs to recover accidentally deleted photos or contacts.

Examples in this book have been provided for both Mac OS X (Leopard) and Microsoft Windows XP. Some general system administration skills (on either platform) will greatly help you get the methods in this book perfected, but these skills are not required. Any difficult command-line work employed in this book will include thorough explanations and examples.

Acknowledgments

Special thanks to the Silicon Valley and North Texas Regional Computer Forensics Laboratory, Evidence Talks, Ltd., Detective Kent Stuart, Agent David Graham, Pepijn Oomen, Youssef Francis, David Wang, and the iPhone Dev Team.

Organization of the Material

Chapter 1, *Introduction to Computer Forensics*, introduces you to digital forensics and its core values and practices.

Chapter 2, *Understanding the iPhone*, introduces you to the iPhone's basic architecture and explains how to get your desktop machine prepared for forensic work.

Chapter 3, *Accessing the iPhone*, explains how to access the iPhone to install an open source forensic toolkit, crack passcode protection, and set up the iPhone to communicate with a desktop on a wireless network.

Chapter 4, *Forensic Recovery*, explains the actual recovery process: how to obtain the raw disk image on the device. It will then introduce you to many recovery tools used to find and carve out deleted files from the iPhone.

Chapter 5, *Electronic Discovery*, explains electronic discovery and shows you what information is available on the live filesystem of the iPhone, and where to find and extract it.

Chapter 6, *Desktop Trace*, illustrates desktop trace: recovering iPhone backups from a desktop and how to prove trusted pairing relationships with a desktop machine.

Chapter 7, *Case Help*, explores various scenarios and what kind of information would be of interest in each case.

The Appendix provides the necessary disclosures and source code for law enforcement agencies, and the information needed to reproduce the methods used in the open source tools employed in this book.

Conventions Used in This Book

The following typographical conventions are used in this book:

Plain text
> Used for menu titles, menu options, menu buttons, and keyboard accelerators.

Italic
> Indicates new terms, URLs, and filenames.

`Constant width`
> Indicates the contents of files, the output from commands, Unix utilities, command-line options, elements of code such as XML tags and SQL names, and generally anything found in programs.

Constant width bold
> Shows commands or other text that should be typed literally by the user, and parts of code or files highlighted to stand out for discussion.

Constant width italic
> Shows text that should be replaced with user-supplied values.

This icon signifies a tip, suggestion, or general note.

This icon indicates a warning or caution.

Using Code Examples

This book is here to help you get your job done. In general, you may use the code in this book in your programs and documentation. You do not need to contact us for permission unless you're reproducing a significant portion of the code. For example, writing a program that uses several chunks of code from this book does not require permission. Selling or distributing a CD-ROM of examples from O'Reilly books *does* require permission. Answering a question by citing this book and quoting example code does not require permission. Incorporating a significant amount of example code from this book into your product's documentation *does* require permission.

We appreciate, but do not require, attribution. An attribution usually includes the title, author, publisher, and ISBN. For example: "*iPhone Forensics*, by Jonathan Zdziarski. Copyright 2008 Jonathan Zdziarski, 978-0-596-15358-8."

If you feel your use of code examples falls outside fair use or the permission given above, feel free to contact us at *permissions@oreilly.com*.

Legal Disclaimer

The technologies discussed in this publication, the limitations on these technologies that the technology and content owners seek to impose, and the laws actually limiting the use of these technologies are constantly changing. Thus, some of the procedures described in this publication may not work, may cause unintended harm to equipment or systems on which they are used, or may be inconsistent with applicable law or user agreements. Your use of these procedures is at your own risk, and O'Reilly Media, Inc. disclaims responsibility for any damage or expense resulting from their use. In any event, you should take care that your use of these procedures does not violate any applicable laws, including copyright laws, and be sure to thoroughly test any procedures before using them on actual evidence.

Safari® Books Online

Safari When you see a Safari® Books Online icon on the cover of your favorite technology book, that means the book is available online through the O'Reilly Network Safari Bookshelf.

Safari offers a solution that's better than e-books. It's a virtual library that lets you easily search thousands of top tech books, cut and paste code samples, download chapters, and find quick answers when you need the most accurate, current information. Try it for free at *http://safari.oreilly.com*.

We'd Like to Hear from You

Please address comments and questions concerning this book to the publisher:

O'Reilly Media, Inc.
1005 Gravenstein Highway North
Sebastopol, CA 95472
800-998-9938 (in the United States or Canada)
707-829-0515 (international or local)
707-829-0104 (fax)

We have a web page for this book, where we list errata, examples, and any additional information. You can access this page at:

http://www.oreilly.com/catalog/9780596153588

To comment or ask technical questions about this book, send email to:

bookquestions@oreilly.com

For more information about our books, conferences, Resource Centers, and the O'Reilly Network, see our website at:

http://www.oreilly.com

 Because the iPhone receives periodic updates from Apple, new techniques are always emerging. Visit the book's website at *http://www.oreilly.com/catalog/9780596153588* for any updates or errata to this book.

## CHAPTER 1

Introduction to Computer Forensics

Forensic science dates back as early as the second century B.C., to Archimedes. Its most modern roots came from the mid to late 1800s, from a man named Henry Faulds. Faulds was a Scottish doctor, archaeologist, and missionary. Discovering fingerprints that had been left in ancient pottery, Faulds published a paper in 1880 suggesting that fingerprints could be used to uniquely identify criminals. This dovetailed the work of William J. Herschel, a British officer stationed in India, who had previously been using fingerprints and handprints as a means of identification on legal notes.

Modern day forensics can be described as the fusion of methodology and science, as it applies to the scientific process of documenting an event or an artifact. As it pertains to criminal and civil court cases, the science and methodology that is performed must adhere to rules of evidence and practices generally accepted within the given legal jurisdiction.

Computer forensics is a branch of forensic science involving the application of science and methodology to preserve, recover, and document electronic evidence. Instead of dealing with dead bodies, examiners in this field deal with dead hard drives. As it pertains to the iPhone, your challenge is even greater in that you will be examining an embedded device, which has been intentionally closed off and was not intended for recovery.

Making Your Search Legal

Before getting started, it's important to emphasize the need for keeping your search legal. In a corporate environment, the company usually has no legal right to seize or examine a personal device belonging to the employee, but can usually examine devices belonging to the company. In corporate investigations, therefore, it's important to verify ownership of the device before performing an examination. Your department should implement an inventory procedure to record the International Mobile Equipment Identity (IMEI) and serial numbers of all corporately owned mobile devices to guarantee ownership prior to examination. Otherwise, your evidence may be ruled inadmissible if criminal charges are filed, and you may even expose the company to a lawsuit.

Law enforcement officers should follow the appropriate steps to acquire a search warrant for the device and desktop machine. The search warrant should specify all electronic information stored on the device including but not limited to text messages, calendar events, photos and videos, caches, logs of recent activity, map and direction queries, map and satellite imagery, personal alarms, notes, music, email, web browsing activity, passwords and personal credentials, fragments of typed communication, voicemail, call history, contacts, information pertaining to relationships with other devices, and items of personal interest.

Rules of Evidence

In both civil and criminal cases, five general rules are used to weigh the value of evidence. These five rules are:

Admissible

> Evidence must have been preserved and gathered in such a way that it can be used in court. Many different errors can be made that could cause a judge to rule a piece of evidence as inadmissible. These can include failure to obtain a proper warrant, breaking the chain of evidence, and mishandling or even destroying the evidence.

Authentic

> The evidence must be relevant to the case, and the forensic examiner must be able to account for the origin of the evidence. For example, intercepting an email transmission is not enough to prove that the alleged sender was responsible for the message. A relationship must be established between the message and the computer it was sent from. It will also need to be established, beyond reasonable doubt, that there was a relationship between the computer, the message, and the person who sent the message.

Complete

> When evidence is presented, it must tell the whole story. A clear and complete picture must be presented that can account for how the evidence came to be. If unchecked, incomplete evidence may go unnoticed, which can be even more dangerous than no evidence at all. As a recent example, consider the case of a man who was charged with possession of child

pornography. The evidence presented showed that the images had been downloaded onto the man's work computer, but it wasn't until much later in the case that the defense revealed that the images had been downloaded by a virus on the machine, and not by the defendant. An innocent man was almost convicted and put in prison because the prosecution's examiner did not present complete evidence—and a jury is not technically savvy enough to see this. With all of the different processes running on a computer, it's critical to be able to tie a piece of evidence to its origins and tell the whole story.

Reliable

Any evidence collected must be reliable. This depends on the methodology and science used. The techniques used must be credible and generally accepted in the field. If the examiner made any errors or used questionable techniques, this could cast reasonable doubt on a case.

Understandable and believable

A forensic examiner must be able to explain, with clarity and conciseness, what processes he used and how the integrity of the evidence was preserved. If the examiner does not appear to understand his own work, a jury may reject it as well. The evidence must be easily explainable and believable.

Good Forensic Practices

As you practice the techniques in this book, keep the following in mind.

Preserve the Evidence

Never work on original copies of evidence. As soon as you recover evidence, create a read-only master copy and check it into a digital vault. All further processing should be performed on copies of the evidence. Since you're dealing with digital evidence, and not old 8-tracks, the copies you make will be identical to the masters. Some tools, if not used properly, can make modifications to the data that's being operated on.

In addition to this, never run any applications on the device until after you've recovered and checked in the evidence. Any time you use the device, something on the disk is likely to be changed. Perform only the tasks that are absolutely necessary, and keep your intrusion into the system minimal.

Document the Evidence

Whenever a master copy is made, use a cryptographic digest such as MD5 to ensure the evidence hasn't been altered in any way. Digests should be stored separately from the data itself, so as to make it even more difficult to tamper with. Digests and proper documentation will help ensure that no cross-contamination has taken place.

In addition to this, document all of the methods you used to collect and extract the evidence. Detail your notes enough that another examiner could reproduce them. This isn't a rule of thumb, but rather is required in many cases. Your work must be reproducible should another forensic examiner challenge your evidence. If your evidence cannot be reproduced, a judge may rule it inadmissible.

Document All Changes

Simply walking into a crime scene destroys evidence—footprints, blood, hairs, and even computer bits can get stomped on when processing the crime scene. It's important to document your entire recovery process, and especially any intentional changes made. For example, if your forensic tool of choice sliced up the disk image to store it, this must be documented. You should document every time you reboot the device, sync it to a desktop case-evidence account, or use an application.

Establish an Investigation Checklist

Every investigation is different, but all should share the same basic recovery and examination practices. Put together a process and create a checklist to dictate how your examinations should be conducted. This will prevent you from forgetting any details, and will also ensure the rest of your team is conducting examinations in the same fashion, so that you can account for others on the stand.

Be Detailed

In addition to this, be detailed to the point of being verbose. It's better to have too many notes than to not have enough. In the courtroom, the opposing attorney will try to discredit you or your evidence. Your case must be rock-solid, and if the attorney can cast doubt by asking you for details you don't recall, you may lose the case. As was already mentioned, your notes must be detailed enough for someone else to reproduce them, but that should be a bare-minimum goal.

Technical Processes

This book covers the following key technical processes:

Physical handling

> The physical handling of the device, prior to its examination. This includes dusting for prints and ensuring you have the right equipment to keep the device charged and connected. You'll also want to remove the SIM card from the device or place the device in a Faraday cage. A Faraday cage is a shielded enclosure that blocks electrical fields, including cellular transmissions.

Establishing communication

> Unlike a desktop machine, where the hard disk can be removed, mobile devices cannot generally be image-processed unless you have special equipment to perform chip dumps. As a result, the device must be "talked to" in order to recover evidence. Establishing communication with the device means setting up the proper physical and network connections to install a forensic toolkit and perform recovery.

Forensic recovery

> The recovery process involves extracting the evidence from the device to create a master copy. This requires special integrity checks to ensure the data hasn't changed between the iPhone and the desktop.

Electronic discovery

> Electronic discovery is the process by which the evidence is processed and analyzed. During this stage, deleted files are recovered and the live filesystem is analyzed. The evidence discovered here will ultimately build an explanation of the evidence that will be delivered through an attorney.

## CHAPTER 2

Understanding the iPhone

Although different models of the iPhone vary, the following core components are commonly found in Apple's first-generation iPhones:

Capability	Equipment
CPU	Samsung/ARM S5L8900B01 512 Mbit SRAM
EDGE	Infineon PMB8876 S-Gold 2 EDGE Baseband Processor
GSM	Infineon M1817A11 GSM RF Transceiver
Disk	Samsung 65-nm 8/16 GB (K9MCG08U5M), 4 GB (K9HBG08U1M) MLC NAND Flash
Amplifier	Skyworks SKY77340-13 Signal Amplifier
Wireless	Marvell 90-nm 88W8686
I/O Controller	Broadcom BCM5973A
Flash Memory	Intel PF38F1030W0YTQ2 (32 MB NOR + 16 MB SRAM)
Audio Processor	Wolfson WM8758
Bluetooth	CSR BlueCore 4
Touchscreen	Philips LPC2221/02992

The iPhone runs a mobile build of Mac OS X 10.5 (Leopard), which has many similarities to its desktop counterpart. The primary differences include:

ARM architecture

> The iPhone uses the ARM (advanced RISC machine) processor architecture, originally developed by ARM Ltd. In contrast, a majority of desktop machines use the Intel x86 architecture.

Hardware

> Special hardware has been added to the iPhone to make it an effective and powerful mobile device. This includes various sensors, such as an accelerometer and proximity sensor, multi-touch capable screen to support

gestures, and of course various radios including GSM, Wi-Fi, and Bluetooth.

User interface frameworks

Apple has built a custom set of user interfaces around the iPhone to accommodate the proprietary hardware sensors and the use of multi-touch. While the desktop version of Leopard contains frameworks for building windows and common controls, the iPhone version of Leopard has replaced these frameworks with a version tailored for creating simple page-like user interfaces, transitions, and finger-friendly controls such as sliders and picker wheels.

Kernel

The iPhone uses a signed kernel, designed to prevent tampering. Many versions of the iPhone kernel have been exploited, however, to serve purposes of *jailbreaking* and *unlocking*.

The hacking community surrounding the iPhone has devised many of the techniques used in this book. In an effort to unlock the device and develop third-party software, the iPhone quickly became the subject of many such hacker groups and developers. Some of these techniques were originally designed to assist in *jailbreaking* the device to allow for third-party software. (The term "jailbreaking" originates from a Unix practice of putting services in a restricted set of directories called a "jail.")

Some of the tools used for jailbreaking overlap with those needed for forensic purposes, and so some of the same tools will be used in this book. Also used will be an open source forensics recovery toolkit for the iPhone consisting of OpenSSH, a basic Unix world, and disk and network copy tools built for the iPhone's ARM architecture using an open source cross-compiler. This will provide you with a template for building more complex toolkits.

What's Stored

While limited portions of personal data can be viewed directly on the iPhone using the GUI interfaces in the iPhone's software, much more hidden and ostensibly deleted data is available by examining the raw disk image, which is why forensic examination of the iPhone is so important. Not only is the live data on the iPhone of interest, but the deleted information can be of even greater benefit. Because a significant amount of personal information is stored in database files, some deleted information remains live on the filesystem, possibly being retained for months or longer.

It is extremely difficult to permanently delete data from an iPhone; however, more recent versions of software have added a secure wipe feature to assist in this process. Many users believe that the iTunes "restore" process formats the device, but in actuality, even this leaves a majority of the old data intact—just not directly visible. In fact, at one time, Apple's own refurbishing process appeared to have taken the iPhone's restore mode for granted: many refurbished devices were reported to contain personal information from the last owner!

Information stored by the iPhone includes:

- Keyboard caches containing usernames, passwords, search terms, and historical fragments of typed communication. Nearly everything typed into the iPhone's keyboard is stored in a keyboard cache, which can linger even after deleted.

- Screenshots are preserved of the last state of an application, taken whenever the home button is pressed or an application is exited. These are used by the iPhone to create aesthetic zoom effects, and often provide several dozen snapshots of user activity.

- Deleted images from the user's photo library, camera roll, and browsing cache can be recovered using a data carving tool.

- Deleted address book entries, contacts, calendar events, and other personal data can often be found in fragments on disk.

- Exhaustive call history, beyond that displayed, is generally available. Approximately the last 100 calls are stored in the call database and can be recovered using a desktop SQLite client. Many deleted entries can also be recovered from deleted sections of the database file using string dumps.

- Map tile images from the iPhone's Google Maps application are preserved as well as direction lookups and longitude/latitude coordinates of previous map searches (including GPS scans). This can be useful when trying to find an individual or associate someone with a location.

- Browser cache and deleted browser objects, which identify the websites a user has visited, can often be recovered.

- Cached and deleted email messages, SMS messages, and other communication can be recovered. Corresponding timestamps and flags are also available to identify with whom and in what direction the communication took place.

- Deleted voicemail recordings often remain on the device. These can be recovered and played through Quicktime or any other audio playback tool supporting the AMR codec.

- Pairing records establishing trusted relationships between the device and one or more desktop computers can be recovered.

Equipment You'll Need

In order to process an iPhone as evidence, you'll need the following:

- A desktop/notebook machine running either Mac OS X Leopard or Windows XP. The tools used in this book are also compatible with Tiger and Vista but are not as widely tested. Examples in this book are provided for both operating systems, so use whichever you're most comfortable with. Due to the compatibility of the iPhone and its native HFS filesystem, however, it is easier to operate on the iPhone's live filesystem using a Leopard-based Mac.

- An iPhone USB dock connector or cable. This will be required to install the forensics recovery toolkit into a nondestructive location on the device and to keep the device charged during the recovery process.

- A working Wi-Fi connection on your desktop machine and an access point to which both the iPhone and the desktop can connect (preferably securely). In the event that you don't have access to an access point that is isolated from other machines on the network, this book also provides instructions for creating an ad-hoc network. In most cases, disk copies can be performed over an SSH tunnel to further secure the data while in transit.

- An implementation of SSH (Secure Shell) on your desktop, including ssh and scp tools. These are part of the OpenSSH package, and can also be found in the free SSH packages at *http://www.ssh.fi.*

- The iTunes software from Apple. Versions 7.6 (for firmware v1.x) and 7.7 (for firmware v2.x) were used for this book, but other versions are likely to work as well. If you're planning on reproducing source code proofs-of-concept, you'll specifically require iTunes version 7.4.2.

- Adequate disk space on the desktop machine to contain copies of the iPhone's media partition and digital vault. The minimum recommended space is three times the device's advertised capacity: one slice for the actual disk image, one slice for a copy to work with, and one slice for digital recovery.

Determining the Firmware Version

If you've already seized a device, you'll want to make sure that its firmware version is supported by the methods in this book. To determine the version of operating firmware installed on the iPhone, tap on the Settings icon, then select General About. The version number will be displayed with a build number in parentheses. Before proceeding, ensure that the firmware version of the device falls within the range of versions supported by this document.

If the device is passcode protected, you will need to circumvent this security measure in order to determine the firmware version. See Chapter 3 for more information.

Never upgrade a device running v1.x firmware to v2.x, or you will destroy evidence. Use the latest version of v1.x software for v1.x devices.

Disk Layout

By default, the iPhone is configured with two disk partitions. These do not reside on a physical disk drive (the type with spinning platters) since the iPhone uses a solid state NAND flash, but are treated as a disk by storing a partition table and formatted filesystem on the flash.

The first partition is a 300 MB system (root) partition used to house the operating system and all of the preloaded applications used with the iPhone. This partition is mounted as read-only by default, and is designed to stay in a factory state for the entire life of the iPhone. The remaining available space is assigned to the user (or "media") partition, which is mounted as */private/var* on the iPhone. This partition is where all of the user data gets written—everything from music to personal contacts. This dual-partition scheme was the most logical way for Apple to perform easy upgrades to the iPhone software, because the first partition can be formatted by iTunes without deleting any of the owner's music or other data.

Because the system partition is intended to remain in a factory state by default, there is no useful evidentiary information that can be obtained from it—it's essentially irrelevant in forensics. The second partition is where all of the useful information resides, and so the first partition is safe for installing forensic tools. The tools used in the coming chapters will be used to remount the system partition as read-write to allow the installation of an open source forensic recovery toolkit. This will be done without changing the behavior of the iPhone or its preloaded applications, and without disturbing user data.

The actual device nodes for the disk are as follows, with the system partition mounted at / and the media partition mounted at */private/var*:

Block devices:

```
brw-r-----  1 root  operator  14,  0 Apr  7 07:46 /dev/disk0    Disk
brw-r-----  1 root  operator  14,  1 Apr  7 07:46 /dev/disk0s1  System
brw-r-----  1 root  operator  14,  2 Apr  7 07:46 /dev/disk0s2  Media
```

Raw devices:

```
crw-r-----  1 root  operator  14,  0 Apr  7 07:46 /dev/rdisk0   Disk
crw-r-----  1 root  operator  14,  1 Apr  7 07:46 /dev/rdisk0s1 System
crw-r-----  1 root  operator  14,  2 Apr  7 07:46 /dev/rdisk0s2 Media
```

Above are the major and minor numbers as well as the default owner and permissions you can expect to encounter for the disk and partition devices on the iPhone. Again, because the system partition is not designed to store user data, this operation is considered to be safe for conducting forensic analysis, as it leaves the media partition (the evidence, and its free space) intact.

Communication

The iPhone can communicate across several different mediums, including the serial port, 802.11 Wi-Fi, and Bluetooth. Due to the limitations of Bluetooth on the iPhone, the two preferred methods are via the serial port and Wi-Fi.

AFC (Apple File Connection) is the serial port protocol used by iTunes to copy files to and from the device and to send firmware-level commands, such as how to boot up and when to enter recovery mode. It is used for everything from copying music to installing a software upgrade. This takes place over the device's USB dock connector, using a framework named MobileDevice, which gets installed with iTunes. Third-party jailbreak tools sometimes load this framework to perform ad-hoc operations on the iPhone.

 A framework is a shared resource used in Mac OS X, similar to a DLL (dynamic linked library) and SO (shared object) in other operating systems. The Windows version of iTunes uses a DLL rather than a framework. For all purposes here, the terms are interchangeable.

By default, iTunes isn't allowed to access the entire iPhone, but is placed in a *jailed* environment. A jailed environment is an environment subordinate to the administrative environment of a system, generally imposing additional restrictions on what resources are accessible. In other words, iTunes is permitted to access only certain files on the iPhone—namely those within its jail rooted in the */private/var/mobile/Media* folder on the device (or */private/var/root/Media* for older versions of the software). The term *jailbreaking* originated from the very first iPhone hacks to break out of this restricted environment, allowing the AFC protocol to read and write files anywhere on the device. The AFC protocol will be used by some of the tools outlined in this book to place the device into recovery mode and, once jailbroken, to install the recovery toolkit on the system partition.

Although AFC is useful for transferring files, it cannot generally read from raw devices, and so will not be used to recover the raw actual disk image from the iPhone when the time comes. Instead, the forensic recovery toolkit will provide all of the tools needed to recover the raw image over Wi-Fi. This allows network tools, such as OpenSSH, to be installed on the device, allowing the examiner to gain shell access directly and perform ad-hoc functions such as generating an MD5 digest of the disk before transmitting it.

With some hacking, the AFC protocol can, in fact, be tricked into transferring raw device data across the serial port, but the procedure is very proprietary and therefore questionable. As a result, it would be difficult for a jury to understand, and the method could be volatile from version to version of the iPhone software. Transferring files over a secure wireless connection is a more widely understood technique, and provides for a more credible level of integrity in recovering the raw device because it uses standard protocols and proper integrity checks.

Upgrading the iPhone Firmware

Apple provides periodic firmware updates for the iPhone that update the operating system, radio baseband, and possibly other device firmware. Thus far, these updates have not resulted in the loss of any live user data, but do frequently rename files and may occasionally write new ones to the media partition. It is therefore advisable not to update the iPhone's firmware for forensic purposes, except as a last resort. You'll have to perform an upgrade only if the device is running an older version of the firmware than is supported by this book (1.0.0 or 1.0.1), and if no other suitable techniques are available to access these older firmware versions in a nondestructive manner.

To upgrade the iPhone firmware to the latest version, use the "update" button available in iTunes. If the most recent version of device firmware is not supported, the closest supported version may be downloaded manually and installed by holding down the Option (Mac) or Shift (Windows) key while clicking the Update button. This will allow the examiner to select the desired firmware file to upgrade to.

This book covers a wide range of iPhone software versions, but you might run into a snag with a particular application if it does not support your version of iPhone software. Do not upgrade the iPhone's firmware unless absolutely necessary. If an upgrade is required, use the closest supported version to the currently installed version.

The following supported iPhone firmware updates can be downloaded from Apple's cache servers:

1.0.2

http://appldnld.apple.com.edgesuite.net/content.info.apple.com/iPhone/ 061-3823.20070821.vormd/iPhone1,1_1.0.2_1C28_Restore.ipsw

1.1.1

http://appldnld.apple.com.edgesuite.net/content.info.apple.com/iPhone/ 061-3883.20070927.In76t/iPhone1,1_1.1.1_3A109a_Restore.ipsw

1.1.2

http://appldnld.apple.com.edgesuite.net/content.info.apple.com/iPhone/ 061-4037.20071107.5Bghn/iPhone1,1_1.1.2_3B48b_Restore.ipsw

1.1.3

http://appldnld.apple.com.edgesuite.net/content.info.apple.com/iPhone/ 061-4061.20080115.4Fvn7/iPhone1,1_1.1.3_4A93_Restore.ipsw

1.1.4

http://appldnld.apple.com.edgesuite.net/content.info.apple.com/iPhone/ 061-4313.20080226.Sw39i/iPhone1,1_1.1.4_4A102_Restore.ipsw

See Apple's iTunes documentation for more information about updating the iPhone firmware.

Restore Mode and Integrity of Evidence

Imagine an employee who has been caught selling corporate secrets. He has just discovered that he is under investigation by the company, and the company's security officers are headed his way to interview him. The first thing he might do is to try and destroy evidence on his iPhone. He presses and holds the Home and Power buttons until the device is forced into recovery mode. Is his data gone? Can it be recovered? What if the employee had a few minutes to initiate a full restore using iTunes?

There are two steps involved in restoring an iPhone: placing the device in *restore mode*, and performing the actual restore with iTunes. In the scenario just described, simply placing the device into restore mode has only stopped the iPhone from booting—and temporarily at that. The "Please Connect to iTunes" display is simply the iPhone's way of saying, "I was told not to boot up, so this is what I'm doing instead." Simply placing a device into restore mode *does not destroy the filesystem*. A forensic examiner may even enter the device into restore mode himself to perform certain tasks such as circumventing passcode protection. If the owner does this, or if a mistake is made during the recovery process leaving the iPhone in recovery mode, *don't panic*. All data still remains intact. The device can in fact be made to boot back into the operating system without a loss of data, provided the user has not initiated the actual restore process (by docking it and invoking a restore through iTunes). The next chapter shows how to reboot the iPhone back into its normal state.

 Some versions of iPhone firmware have been reported to kick themselves out of recovery mode within ten minutes of sitting idle while connected to the dock.

Let's say the worst has occurred: the employee had the time to initiate a restore through iTunes and the device is being formatted. The first thing you should do is *let the process complete*. The only thing more dangerous to data than destroying the filesystem on the iPhone is to undock it while it's in the process. When fully restored to its factory state, the filesystem is in fact destroyed; however, the disk is not wiped. This means that most of the data that was previously on the iPhone should still be recoverable. You will need to use a *data-carving tool* such as Scalpel to carve the now-deleted data out of the raw disk image. This is covered in Chapter 4.

 You may also be able to retrieve some important files from the device backups stored on the suspect's desktop machine. See Chapter 6 for more information.

To summarize, placing the iPhone into recovery mode does nothing significant, and the iPhone can be easily booted back into normal operating mode. Performing a full restore via iTunes will destroy the live filesystem but will not wipe the disk, leaving most of the evidence intact, but slightly more difficult to get to.

 The only time you should consider interrupting a restore process is when the user has initiated a secure wipe using v2.x firmware. When this occurs, the Apple logo is displayed with a thermometer. Use the instructions in Chapter 3 to place the device in Device Failsafe Utility (DFU) so that it can be recovered later.

Cross-Contamination and Syncing

The last thing you should know before you get started is that the iPhone likes to sync data, and this can present a risk of cross-contamination. When the iPhone syncs to a desktop, it can copy the desktop's address book, photos, music, and other data. The desktop can also copy its own data back to the iPhone. Therefore, before performing any of the steps in the coming chapters, be sure to disable all automatic syncing in order to keep the iPhone's current data pristine:

1. Open iTunes on the desktop machine.
2. Select Preferences from the iTunes menu.
3. Click on the Syncing tab.
4. Check the box next to "Disable automatic syncing for all iPhones and iPods." This is illustrated in Figure 2-1.

Figure 2-1. iTunes preferences with automatic syncing disabled

 As an alternative, consider using a bootable CD or virtual machine to perform the recovery steps outlined throughout the rest of this book.

In addition to this procedure, it's also a good idea to conduct all of your forensic recovery and examination using a desktop machine with a separate user account for each case. Think of a user account as an "evidence box"—you wouldn't consider putting evidence from two different cases in the same box! Ensure that you have created and are logged into a separate, nonprivileged user account. When using Mac OS X, the user account may also be encrypted with file vault to prevent cross-contamination between nonadministrative accounts.

 Never attempt to sync a suspect's device manually unless it is with a new, nonprivileged user account designated specifically for the case at hand.

The Takeaway

A whole lot of personal activity is stored on the iPhone, and much of this is useful for evidence. Your investigation should produce useful evidence if you remember the following:

- The iPhone has two partitions: one for the operating system and one for user data. The user data partition is the only one that matters.
- The forensic recovery toolkit is installed using the USB cable, but the actual recovery takes place over Wi-Fi. You'll need Wi-Fi on your desktop machine.
- Some versions of iPhone software are too old to work with this book, requiring an upgrade. The upgrade process generally does little (if any) damage to evidence, but should only be performed when necessary.
- Placing the device into restore mode does not destroy any data, and the iPhone can be booted back into normal mode easily.
- Performing a full restore via iTunes destroys the filesystem, but leaves most of the evidence recoverable by a data-carving tool, as explained in Chapter 4.
- Use separate, nonprivileged user accounts on the desktop machine to prevent cross-contamination, and never sync a device outside of such an account.

## CHAPTER 3

Accessing the iPhone

After reading the earlier chapters of this book, you should have a rudimentary understanding of how the iPhone functions on an operating system level, and should have created a secure environment to work on your desktop without the risk of cross-contamination. In this chapter, you'll install the forensic recovery toolkit—an open source toolkit containing tools for recovering the raw disk image of the iPhone. While some example toolkits have been provided online to complement this book, all payload and staging files are simple zip archives. This means you can easily replace the standard toolkit with your own tools, which can be compiled for the iPhone using a publicly available open source tool chain. Instructions for setting up the tool chain can be found on Jay Freeman's website: *http://www.saurik.com/id/4.*

Whether you use the stock recovery tools or build your own, these tools will be the means by which you'll gain access to the device's operating system. You'll access the device by installing a forensic-friendly jailbreak tool that safeguards against writes to the user partition of the device. This will, in turn, install an SSH daemon on the iPhone, allowing you to access it over a secure network connection.

Installing the Recovery Toolkit (Firmware v1.0.2–1.1.4)

The iLiberty+ program is a free tool designed by Youssef Francis and Pepijn Oomen for unlocking the iPhone/iPod and installing various payloads onto the iPhone/iPod Touch. Under normal circumstances, the iPhone's built-in digital signing mechanism will allow only firmware that has been signed by Apple to be installed. iLiberty+ takes advantage of a loophole in the v1.x firmware and instructs the iPhone's kernel to boot an unsigned RAM disk. This allows for software that is otherwise unsanctioned by Apple to be booted out of the iPhone's memory. The RAM disk used by iLiberty+ contains a proprietary payload delivery system, which has been enhanced to safely install our forensic toolkit payload onto the device.

The default payload allows the media partition to be accessed through the user interface, which is preferred for most examinations.

The recovery toolkit includes:

- A basic Unix world
- OpenSSH, a secure shell
- The netcat tool, for sending data across a network
- The md5 tool, for creating a cryptographic digest of the disk image
- The dd disk copy/image tool, used to access the disk device

For a low-level explanation of the technical procedures used by this tool, see the "Technical Procedure" section in the Appendix.

Step 1: Download and Install iLiberty+

Download the latest version of iLiberty+ from *http://theiphoneproject.org*. Archives of the versions used in this book may also be downloaded from the O'Reilly website at *http://www.oreilly.com/9780596153588*.

iLiberty+ version 1.6 or greater is recommended, especially for law enforcement purposes. Version 1.6 corrects problems with inadvertent (yet minor) writing to the user data partition present in version 1.51. It also adds compatibility with certain older versions of iPhone software.

Mac OS X (iLiberty+ v1.6)

Extract the contents of the archive and drag the iLiberty+ application into your */Applications* folder.

Windows (iLiberty+ v1.3.0.113)

Run the iLiberty+ installer application. The application will be installed in *C:\Program Files\iLiberty*, and icons will be added to the desktop and/or Start Menu.

Step 2: Dock the iPhone and Launch iTunes

Connect the iPhone to its dock connector and the other end to your desktop's USB port. This will keep the device charged during the recovery process and provide the serial connection needed to install the toolkit. Once connected, launch iTunes from the desktop and ensure the device is recognized. The iPhone should appear on the iTunes sidebar under the Devices section.

 If the device was seized while in restore mode, iTunes will list the device to be in recovery mode. *Do not perform a recovery*, but instead follow the steps in the next section to boot the device out of recovery mode.

Step 3: Launch iLiberty+ and Verify Connectivity

Launch iLiberty+. The iPhone should be detected upon launch.

 During the jailbreaking process, iTunes may notify you that it has detected a device in recovery mode and prompt you to restore it. This is normal, as iTunes is oblivious to the fact that the device is being accessed by another application. *Never instruct iTunes to perform a restore, or you will damage evidence!* If necessary, you may cancel this request or simply ignore it.

Booting out of recovery mode

If the device was seized while in restore mode, it may not be immediately detected by iLiberty+. Choose the Exit Recovery option from iLiberty+'s Advanced menu (Mac OS X) or the Jump Out of Recovery Mode option from the Other Tools tab (Windows) to boot the device back into the operating system. The device should boot within 20 seconds. Other tools, such as iBrickr, iNdependence, and iPHUC (iPHone Utility Client) can also be used to boot the iPhone if the iLiberty+ method should fail. In some cases, the iPhone will kick itself out of recovery mode after approximately 10 minutes, provided it remains powered on and connected to iTunes through the USB dock cable.

Verify that the iPhone has been detected by looking at the device description in iLiberty+.

Mac OS X

Click on the Device Info tab to view information about the device's system and media partitions (Figure 3-1).

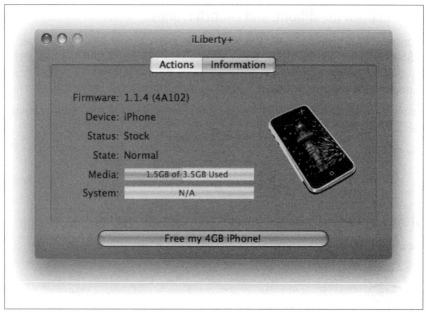

Figure 3-1. iLiberty+ device status (Mac OS X)

Windows

Verify that iLiberty+ is reporting the status of the iPhone at the bottom right of the status bar. The status should read Normal Mode (see Figure 3-2).

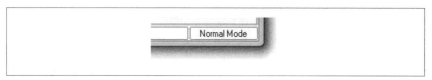

Figure 3-2. iLiberty+ device status (Windows)

Step 4: Activate the Forensic Toolkit Payload

After the iPhone has been recognized by iLiberty+, the forensic recovery payload may be downloaded and activated for installation within iLiberty+. Releases of the toolkit are stored in a repository located on O'Reilly's website, along with additional tools and example payloads. You can build your own tools by simply following the iLiberty+ payload creation documentation, or mimicking the layout of our examples. Our recovery toolkit includes OpenSSH, netcat, and some other open source utilities. Each version of the toolkit is distributed in both *.lby* format (for Mac OS X) and *.zip* file format (for Windows). The two archives are identical: they simply use different file

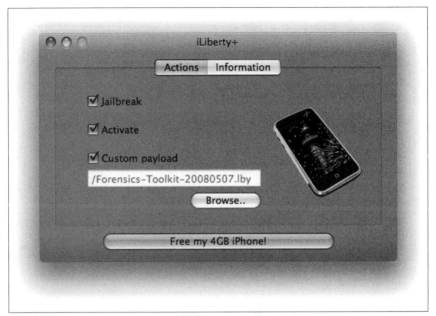

Figure 3-3. Selecting forensic toolkit payload (Mac OS X)

extensions. Download the appropriate file extension for your operating system.

 Some web browsers will automatically rename the .lby file to have a .zip file extension. If you are unable to select your payload in iLiberty+, check to ensure that the file extension is correct, and rename it back to .lby if necessary.

Mac OS X

Click on the Actions tab in iLiberty+. Make sure all payload checkboxes are unchecked. Check the checkbox labeled "Select a custom payload manually" (Figure 3-3). Download the latest (or desired) version of the forensic toolkit payload .lby file from the O'Reilly website and then click Browse. Locate the file and click Open. It should now be selected and displayed in the custom payload field.

 Be sure to disable Safari's option to "Open safe files after downloading," or Safari will attempt to extract the contents of the payload.

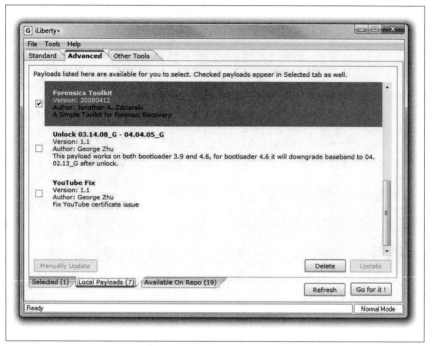

Figure 3-4. Selecting forensics toolkit payload (Windows)

Windows

Unlike the Mac version of iLiberty+, the recovery payload needs to be extracted in Windows. Download the latest version of the forensic toolkit payload *.zip* file from the previously mentioned URL. Extract the contents of the archive into a directory. This should output two files: *90Forensics.sh* and *forensics-toolkit-(VERSION).zip*. Copy or move these two files into *C:\Program Files\iLiberty\payload*.

Now click the Advanced tab. Click the bottom tab titled Local Payloads. Scroll to the forensics toolkit payload and click its checkbox (Figure 3-4). The payload should then appear under the Selected tab, which means it is now activated for installation.

 If the toolkit does not appear on the list of local payloads, try clicking the Refresh button or restart iLiberty+.

Step 5: Install the Payload

After verifying that the forensics toolkit payload has been activated, execute the jailbreak and payload installation.

Mac OS X

Click "Free my iPhone" at the bottom of the window. A window will appear informing you of iLiberty+'s progress. The iPhone should boot into a text-based screen and install the toolkit payload.

Windows

Click "Go for It" at the bottom of the window. Before the jailbreak process commences, you will be asked to unplug the iPhone from its USB connection and then reconnect it. Unplug the device, and wait until it disappears from iTunes. Reconnect the device, and wait until it appears again in iTunes. Only after this, click the OK button.

A progress window will appear, but may vanish as the device enters recovery mode. The process is still running in the background, however, and you should see status text such as "Booting Ramdisk" in the status bar of the iLiberty+ application. The device itself should, after a short time, boot into a text-based screen to install the toolkit payload.

It's stuck!

In rare cases, the device will either get stuck in recovery mode or fail to enter recovery mode at all. Recover as follows:

- If the device becomes stuck in recovery mode, follow the instructions in step 2 to boot the device back into the operating system. This will safely boot the device without any loss of data.
- If the device fails to enter recovery mode (appearing to do nothing), manually force it into recovery by holding down the Power and Home buttons until the device hard-powers itself off, powers itself back on, and finally displays the recovery screen (do not let up on the buttons until you see the "Connect to iTunes" text and/or icon). In iLiberty+, click the Manual Boot option on the Other Tools tab to boot the device manually. The device will boot out of recovery and install the forensics toolkit payload. Should this fail, repeat steps 2–5 once more.

What to watch for

During the jailbreak process, the iPhone itself will go through what will appear to be various text-based diagnostic and configuration screens. During the process, you should see SSH keys being generated. Note any errors, should they occur. Once the process has completed, the device should briefly display the message "Forensics Toolkit Installation Successful" and will then reboot back into its operational state.

The device should now be ready to accept an SSH connection. You're ready to configure Wi-Fi and perform recovery.

Circumventing Passcode Protection (Firmware v1.0.2– 1.1.4)

The iPhone uses two types of locks: a SIM lock and an OS-level passcode. When the passcode is active, the iPhone cannot be synced or accessed

The SIM lock can be bypassed by simply removing or replacing the protected SIM card. This section shows how to bypass the OS-level passcode. The forensic toolkit cannot be installed while either form of protections is active.

The procedures in this section disable the passcode by issuing raw commands to the iPhone to load a specially crafted RAM disk. This custom RAM disk moves the configuration file for passcode protection safely out of the way. When the iPhone boots, it will see that this configuration file is missing and fail over to its default mode of operation, which doesn't require a passcode. Neat, huh?

Automated Bypass

Newer versions of iLiberty+ support a "Bypass Passcode" feature integrated right into the software. To use this, the device will need to be placed into a clean recovery state:

1. Cleanly power the device down by holding the Power button until the "Slide to Power Off" slider appears. Slide this to power off the device.

2. After the device is powered down, press and briefly hold the Power button, then immediately release it when the iPhone appears to be powering on.

3. After releasing the Power button, press and hold both the Power and Home buttons until the device again power cycles and the restore logo is displayed.

4. After the device is in recovery mode, make sure it is connected to the dock and launch iLiberty+. Select "Bypass Passcode" from iLiberty+'s Advanced menu, as shown in Figure 3-5. On a Mac, this will be at the top of the screen.

Figure 3-5. iLiberty+ "Bypass Passcode" menu item

The device should reboot and go through a passcode removal process. When the process is complete, the iPhone will boot back into normal mode and should no longer require a passcode. If this technique fails, try repeating all the steps. It's very important that the device be cleanly powered down; otherwise, the RAM disk won't be able to mount the filesystem.

If this technique persistently fails, try the manual bypass described next.

Manual Bypass

To manually bypass passcode protection, you will require the use of an open source tool called the iPhone Utility Client (humorously named iPHUC).

- The Mac OS X version of this tool can be found at *http://code.google.com/ p/iphuc*.

- The Windows version of this tool can be found at *http://code.google.com/ p/iphucwin32*.

Follow the instructions in the archive to prepare an environment using the correct readline and iTunes Mobile Device dynamic libraries, and install the utility client.

Step 1: Prepare a custom RAM disk

You'll need to prepare a custom RAM disk to move the device's configuration files out of the way, effectively bypassing the passcode. The easiest way to do this is to modify the RAM disk included with iLiberty+, using a hex editor to add a few simple shell commands to its process:

1. Download the Mac version of iLiberty+ 1.51 from *http://theiphoneproject .org*. Do this even if you aren't using a Mac. Extract the application from the archive.

2. Browse inside the *iLiberty+.app* application folder. If you're on a Mac, you can Ctrl-click on the application and choose Show Package Contents from the pop-up menu. You will find a file named *iLiberty+.bin* inside *iLiberty+.app/Contents/Resources/*. Copy this file to a safe location and rename it *iLiberty+.zip*.

3. Extract the contents of *iLiberty+.zip*. The password to the archive is `LittleBear4A102`. This will output a file named *sunny.bin*, which is iLiberty+'s default RAM disk, used to install payloads onto a device.

4. Using Hex Fiend, HexEdit 32, or some other hex editor, edit the file *sunny.bin*. Use the editor's **overwrite** mode to write in the following shell code at offset 0x007DC661. Then save the file. This is your modified RAM disk image. The resulting file should look similar to Figure 3-6 and will contain the shell code you just typed in:

```
nvram auto-boot=true.nvram -d boot-args
fsck_hfs -fy /dev/disk0s1 > /dev/null 2>&1
/sbin/mount_hfs -o noasync,sync /dev/disk0s1 /mnt1
/sbin/mount_hfs -o noasync,sync /dev/disk0s2 /tmp
mv /tmp/mobile/Library/Preferences /tmp/Prefs.mobile
mv /tmp/root/Library/Preferences /tmp/Prefs.root
echo "RELOACATED PREFERENCES"
sleep 30
reboot
```

Step 2: Enter recovery mode

Use the following steps to place the device into a clean recovery mode:

1. Power the device down by holding the Power button until the "Slide to Power Off" slider appears. Slide this to power off the device.

2. After the device is powered down, press and briefly hold the Power button, then immediately release it when the iPhone appears to be powering on.

3. After releasing the Power button, press and hold both Power and Home buttons until the device again power cycles and the restore logo is displayed. If done correctly, this should happen before the device's home screen (springboard) appears.

Step 3: Upload and boot the custom bypass RAM disk

Launch iPHUC from the command line. You should see "Device Connected in Recovery Mode" followed by a recovery prompt. This means you are connected to a type of recovery console in iPHUC, which can be used to send raw commands to the iPhone.

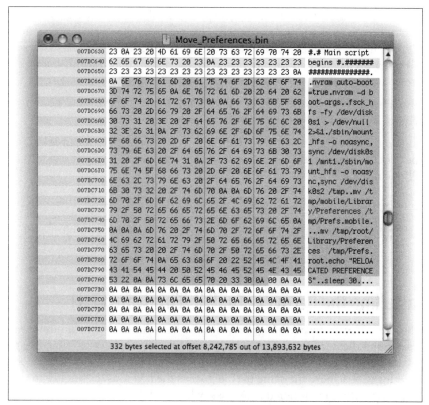

```
007DC630  23 0A 23 20 4D 61 69 6E 20 73 63 72 69 70 74 20  #.# Main script
007DC640  62 65 67 69 6E 73 20 23 0A 23 23 23 23 23 23 23  begins #.#######
007DC650  23 23 23 23 23 23 23 23 23 23 23 23 23 23 23 0A  ##############.
007DC660  0A 6E 76 72 61 6D 20 61 75 74 6F 2D 62 6F 6F 74  .nvram auto-boot
007DC670  3D 74 72 75 65 0A 6E 76 72 61 6D 20 2D 64 20 62  =true.nvram -d b
007DC680  6F 6F 74 2D 61 72 67 73 0A 0A 66 73 63 6B 5F 68  oot-args..fsck_h
007DC690  66 73 20 2D 66 79 20 2F 64 65 76 2F 64 69 73 6B  fs -fy /dev/disk
007DC6A0  30 73 31 20 3E 20 2F 64 65 76 2F 6E 75 6C 6C 20  0s1 > /dev/null
007DC6B0  32 3E 26 31 0A 2F 73 62 69 6E 2F 6D 6F 75 6E 74  2>&1./sbin/mount
007DC6C0  5F 68 66 73 20 2D 6F 20 6E 6F 61 73 79 6E 63 2C  _hfs -o noasync,
007DC6D0  73 79 6E 63 20 2F 64 65 76 2F 64 69 73 6B 30 73  sync /dev/disk0s
007DC6E0  31 20 2F 6D 6E 74 31 0A 2F 73 62 69 6E 2F 6D 6F  1 /mnt1./sbin/mo
007DC6F0  75 6E 74 5F 68 66 73 20 2D 6F 20 6E 6F 61 73 79  unt_hfs -o noasy
007DC700  6E 63 2C 73 79 6E 63 20 2F 64 65 76 2F 64 69 73  nc,sync /dev/dis
007DC710  6B 30 73 32 20 2F 74 6D 70 0A 0A 6D 76 20 2F 74  k0s2 /tmp..mv /t
007DC720  6D 70 2F 6D 6F 62 69 6C 65 2F 4C 69 62 72 61 72  mp/mobile/Librar
007DC730  79 2F 50 72 65 66 65 72 65 6E 63 65 73 20 2F 74  y/Preferences /t
007DC740  6D 70 2F 50 72 65 66 73 2E 6D 6F 62 69 6C 65 0A  mp/Prefs.mobile.
007DC750  0A 0A 0A 6D 76 20 2F 74 6D 70 2F 72 6F 6F 74 2F  ...mv /tmp/root/
007DC760  4C 69 62 72 61 72 79 2F 50 72 65 66 65 72 65 6E  Library/Preferen
007DC770  63 65 73 20 20 2F 74 6D 70 2F 50 72 65 66 73 2E  ces  /tmp/Prefs.
007DC780  72 6F 6F 74 0A 65 63 68 6F 20 22 52 45 4C 4F 41  root.echo "RELOA
007DC790  43 41 54 45 44 20 50 52 45 46 45 52 45 4E 45 45  CATED PREFERENEE
007DC7A0  53 22 0A 0A 73 6C 65 65 70 20 33 30 0A 00 0A 0A  S"..sleep 30....
007DC7B0  0A 0A 0A 0A 0A 0A 0A 0A 0A 0A 0A 0A 0A 0A 0A 0A  ................
007DC7C0  0A 0A 0A 0A 0A 0A 0A 0A 0A 0A 0A 0A 0A 0A 0A 0A  ................
007DC7D0  0A 0A 0A 0A 0A 0A 0A 0A 0A 0A 0A 0A 0A 0A 0A 0A  ................
007DC7E0  0A 0A 0A 0A 0A 0A 0A 0A 0A 0A 0A 0A 0A 0A 0A 0A  ................
007DC7F0  0A 0A 0A 0A 0A 0A 0A 0A 0A 0A 0A 0A 0A 0A 0A 0A  ................
```

332 bytes selected at offset 8,242,785 out of 13,893,632 bytes

Figure 3-6. Modified sunny.bin file containing passcode circumvention

Issue the following commands to upload and boot the passcode circumvention tool. Be sure to escape the spaces with backslashes as shown. The output is shown along with your commands:

```
$ ./iPHUC
(iPHUC Recovery) #: filecopytophone sunny.bin
filecopytophone: 0
(iPHUC Recovery) #: cmd setenv\ boot-args\ rd=md0\ -x\ -s\ pmd0=0x9340000.
0xA00000
(iPHUC Recovery) #: cmd saveenv
(iPHUC Recovery) #: cmd bootx
(iPHUC Recovery) #: exit
```

The iPhone will now boot into verbose mode. The passcode shell code will be invoked and move the configuration files on the device into */private/var/ Prefs.root* and */private/var/Prefs.mobile*. Among these files is the iPhone's home screen (springboard) configuration file, normally found in the preferences folder, found here: */private/var/mobile/Library/Preferences/com.ap ple.springboard.plist*. This property list contains the user's passcode preferences, which default to having no passcode. The file is moved to */private/ var* for later examination, if so desired. This preserves the original preferences file, but upon reboot causes the iPhone to default to having no passcode set. All other preferences are also removed to avoid any conflicts with the user's previous iPhone behavior settings.

The iPhone will reboot itself back into normal mode, and should no longer require a passcode.

Should the device fail to boot the RAM disk, retry step 3, but instead of issuing the `bootx` command, use `fsboot` instead. This may work on older versions of iPhone firmware.

 If you see errors concerning `mount_hfs`, this suggests that the device was not cleanly shut down. Try powering the device off properly using the "Slide to Power Off" method and then, when it powers on, force the device into recovery mode.

Installing the Recovery Toolkit (Firmware v2.x)

The latest v2.x firmware changed much about how the iPhone communicates, warranting the need for a different approach to "owning" (or as some like to say, "pwning") the firmware in order to install a recovery toolkit. The methods used for v2.x achieve the same overall goal as the previous techniques in this chapter: booting an unsigned RAM disk, which installs a recovery toolkit. The mechanism by which this is delivered, however, has changed considerably.

The procedure for v2.x involves taking advantage of a vulnerability in the iPhone's boot ROM that allows it to accept unsigned firmware upgrades. A popular tool known as Pwnage exploits this vulnerability and builds a custom firmware package. Normally, this would destroy the filesystem on the iPhone, so before restoring the firmware, you'll use another tool named Xpwn to modify the firmware "restore" to act as more of an "upgrade" to install your recovery payload. Thus, the procedure will install both the recovery toolkit and a patched operating system kernel, which is needed in order to run unsigned applications. The steps are rather involved, but once you've assembled the proper firmware bundles, you'll be able to easily reuse them for future examinations. The overall plan follows:

1. Use Pwnage to hack the boot ROM on the iPhone and build a custom firmware package. At the time of this writing, all iPhones on the market are supported by Pwnage, and newer device models are generally added within a few weeks.

2. Use Xpwn to create a "Stage 1" customized firmware bundle that will upgrade the NOR (kernel cache) without destroying live data.

3. Use Xpwn to create a "Stage 2" customized firmware bundle that will install the forensic recovery toolkit.

4. Install each customized firmware through iTunes with the iPhone in DFU mode to gain access to the iPhone.

Unlike the techniques for older firmware, the recovery toolkit for v2.x also incorporates built-in passcode removal. This will install the recovery toolkit, reset the iPhone's root password to `alpine`, and remove any passcode protection in one set of operations.

Step 1: Install and Run Pwnage v2.x

Pwnage is a tool designed and written by a group of hackers known as the iPhone Dev Team. It attempts to "own" the iPhone by modifying the boot loader to accept any firmware the user desires to feed it. This allows third-party modifications and lets anyone truly customize Apple's firmware prior to installation. A version of Pwnage that runs on OS X can be downloaded from the Dev Team website at *http://www.iphone-dev.org*. A Windows version, WinPwn, is also available at *http://www.winpwn.com*.

Download and install Pwnage. Before running it, you'll want to make sure you've downloaded the firmware for the appropriate device. If the device is a first-generation iPhone, the firmware's prefix should be *iPhone1,1*. For second-generation (3G) iPhones, the firmware's prefix should be *iPhone1,2*.

Upon launching Pwnage, you'll be prompted for the type of device you have, as shown in Figure 3-7. Be sure to choose the correct device, as attempting to run Pwnage on the wrong device might permanently damage the unit. After you've selected your device, click the Expert Mode button at the top, and then the Next arrow to proceed to the following page.

You'll next be prompted to choose the version of firmware you'd like to use with the device. Be sure the firmware version matches the current version running on the device. If Pwnage is unable to locate your firmware, you may need to download it from Apple's servers. The following firmware downloads are hosted by Apple's cache partners. Alternatively, links to backup caches of various firmware bundles can be found using a search engine:

First-generation iPhones running v2.0

- *http://appldnld.apple.com.edgesuite.net/content.info.apple.com/iPhone/ 061-4956.20080710.V50OI/iPhone1,1_2.0_5A347_Restore.ipsw*

Figure 3-7. Pwnage device selection screen

- *http://appldnld.apple.com.edgesuite.net/content.info.apple.com/iPhone/
  061-5135.20080729.Vfgtr/iPhone1,1_2.0.1_5B108_Restore.ipsw*

- *http://appldnld.apple.com.edgesuite.net/content.info.apple.com/iPhone/
  061-5246.20080818.2V0hO/iPhone1,1_2.0.2_5C1_Restore.ipsw*

3G iPhones running v2.0

- *http://appldnld.apple.com.edgesuite.net/content.info.apple.com/iPhone/
  061-4955.20080710.bgt53/iPhone1,2_2.0_5A347_Restore.ipsw*

- *http://appldnld.apple.com.edgesuite.net/content.info.apple.com/iPhone/
  061-5134.20080729.Q2W3E/iPhone1,2_2.0.1_5B108_Restore.ipsw*

- *http://appldnld.apple.com.edgesuite.net/content.info.apple.com/iPhone/
  061-5241.20080818.t5Fv3/iPhone1,2_2.0.2_5C1_Restore.ipsw*

A complete list of firmware links can be found at *http://www.modmyifone.com/
wiki/index.php/IPhone_Firmware_Download_Links*.

After selecting the appropriate firmware version, you'll go to an advanced customization screen, where you can choose which options should be enabled in the custom firmware bundle. Double-click the General tab, and you will be guided through the various pages of options. The important ones you'll want to be concerned with are:

Activation

This automatically activates the device so that you don't need a valid SIM to access the user interface. When activation is "hacked" in this fashion, the device will generally fail to operate on the carrier's network. If you still require that the device be able to make and receive calls, uncheck this box. Disabling the service in this fashion can be a useful side effect for forensic examination. Restoring back to the original firmware will undo this action.

Restore images

By default, custom restore images are built into the firmware bundle. These are useful only for troubleshooting, and it is recommended that you uncheck these options. If you do keep them, they will be removed by restoring the original firmware.

Accept defaults for the remaining options. When you have completed all of the settings pages, you'll be returned to the main screen. Double-click the Build button and click the Next arrow, as shown in Figure 3-8.

Custom package settings

When prompted for custom package installers, uncheck all installers, including Cydia and the generic "Installer." This will prevent any third-party package installers from being added to the iPhone.

A custom firmware bundle will be stored on your desktop. *Do not install this.* You're going to use this only as the foundation for your custom recovery packages.

Once the custom firmware bundle has been built, you'll be asked if the device has ever been "Pwned" before. Unless you are certain that it has been, click No. You will then be walked through the process of placing the iPhone into Device Failsafe Utility (DFU) mode, at which point it will have its boot ROM modified to accept unsigned firmware.

Once the process has completed, Pwnage will prompt you to quit and restore through iTunes. Quit Pwnage, but *do not restore at this time* through iTunes. The next steps build the actual firmware you restore with, which won't be destructive to the live filesystem.

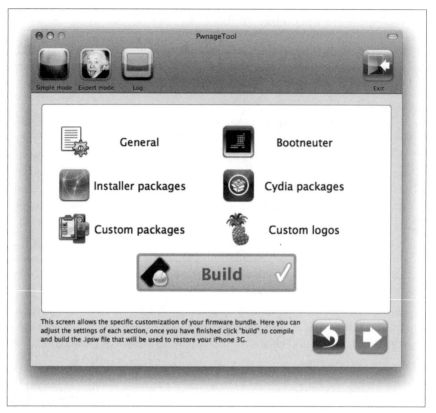

Figure 3-8. Pwnage settings screen

Step 2: Use Xpwn to Customize the Stage 1 Firmware

After completing step 1, you'll have a firmware file stored on your desktop with a name like *iPhone1,2_2.0_5A347_Custom_Restore.ipsw*. By default, restoring with this file would destroy the contents of your filesystem and install a new, fresh copy of jailbroken iPhone software. Instead, you'll use the Xpwn tool to create a custom bundle based on this firmware, which will act as a firmware "upgrade" rather than a restore. By the time you're finished, installing the firmware will only modify the root filesystem of the device without changing the media partition, and will preserve the live filesystem of both partitions.

Xpwn is an open source tool written by David Wang (also known as "planetbeing") and is designed to manage the proprietary img3 format in which RAM disks are packed. Xpwn can run on Linux, Windows, and Mac OS X. Download and install the correct version of Xpwn from *http://wikee*

.iphwn.org/news:xpwn_release. Archives of Xpwn may also be downloaded from the online book examples.

The only utility you'll be using from the Xpwn package is called xpwntool. This is the actual RAM disk management tool that will allow you to unpack and then repack the RAM disk.

Before proceeding, obtain root privileges to ensure file ownership and permissions are retained.

You'll need a few custom directories to work in: one to contain the Pwnage firmware bundle and one to contain your modified "stage 1" bundle. Create the directories and then extract the contents of the custom firmware into each.

Be sure to use the custom firmware bundle created by Pwnage, as the original firmware provided by Apple will not allow the modifications you'll be making to run.

```
# mkdir firmware
# mkdir stage1
# unzip -d firmware ~/Desktop/iPhone1,2_2.0_5A347_Custom_Restore.ipsw
# unzip -d stage1 ~/Desktop/iPhone1,2_2.0_5A347_Custom_Restore.ipsw
```

The *firmware* folder should remain unchanged from here on in. You'll need to refer to it occasionally to get copies of the unmodified files.

Inside the *stage1* folder, you'll see two files ending with a *.dmg* extension. The smaller of these files is the firmware's RAM disk. In this example, the file is named *018-3783-2.dmg*:

```
# ls -l stage1
drwx------   4 root  staff        136 Jun 25 23:23 .fseventsd
-rw-r--r--   1 root  staff  220221811 Jul 24 19:15 018-3782-2.dmg
-rw-r--r--   1 root  staff   26217752 Jul 26 00:57 018-3783-2.dmg
drwxr-xr-x   4 root  staff        136 Jun 25 23:29 Firmware
-rw-r--r--   1 root  staff       1668 Jun 26 00:09 Restore.plist
-rw-r--r--   1 root  staff    3863239 Jul 24 19:12 kernelcache.release.
s5l8900x
```

In order to mount the RAM disk, you'll need to first unpack it, which requires that you obtain its encryption key and initialization vector. All of the versions of iPhone firmware supported by Xpwn can be found in Xpwn's *Firmware Bundles* folder, generally installed in */usr/local*. Locate the *FirmwareBundles* bundle directory at the location you installed Xpwn and find a subdirectory matching the filename of your firmware. Open the *Info.plist* property list contained inside this directory. As you scroll the file, you'll find the filename of the RAM disk followed by a key and initialization vector (called the IV). An example is shown here:

```
<key>Restore Ramdisk</key>
            <dict>
                        <key>File</key>
                        <string>018-3783-2.dmg</string>
                        <key>Patch</key>
                        <string>018-3783-2.patch</string>
                        <key>Patch2</key>
                        <string>018-3783-2-nowipe.patch</string>
                        <key>IV</key>
                        <string>a9681f625d1f61271ec3116601b8bcde</string>
                        <key>Key</key>
                        <string>750afc271132d15ae6989565567e65bf</string>
                        <key>TypeFlag</key>
                        <integer>8</integer>
            </dict>
```

You've now got everything you need to unpack and decrypt the RAM disk. Use xpwntool, as shown below, to decrypt the RAM disk into a file named *stage1-decrypted.dmg*:

```
# xpwntool ./stage1/018-3783-2.dmg ./stage1-decrypted.dmg -k encryption_key \
-iv initialization_vector
```

Once the operation completes, the new file will contain an HFS filesystem, which can be mounted in read-write mode. On Mac OS X, use the hdid tool, as shown below. If using Windows, you'll need to use a tool such as MacDrive, in Target Disk mode.

```
# hdid -readwrite ./stage1-decrypted.dmg
```

The file will be mounted in */Volumes/ramdisk* on Mac OS X Leopard, or wherever you specify using tools on other operating systems. Use the *stage1-prep.zip* archive from our examples to replace the newfs_hfs and fdisk binaries with the contents of Unix */bin/true*. This causes any attempts to format or restructure the filesystem to gracefully fail. Because you'll be working with the custom copy of the firmware provided by Pwnage, it won't be necessary to back up any of the binaries you overwrite. The prep package also modifies the restore options to avoid creating new partitions, and adds to additional libraries as needed.

```
# unzip -od /Volumes/ramdisk /path/to/stage1-prep.zip
```

The following files will have been changed on the RAM disk:

```
./sbin/newfs_hfs
./usr/lib/libintl.8.0.2.dylib
./usr/lib/libintl.8.dylib
./usr/lib/libintl.dylib
./usr/lib/libintl.la
```

```
./usr/local/share/restore/options.plist
./usr/sbin/fdisk
```

Once the operation is complete, unmount the RAM disk:

```
# hdiutil unmount /Volumes/ramdisk
```

Use Xpwn to repack the decrypted RAM disk back into the correct format, and overwrite the old one. For clarification, the example below refers to three files in the following order: the decrypted source image that you just modified, the target image you'll actually use in your firmware bundle, and a "template" image, which is the original RAM disk created with the Pwnage-customized firmware bundle. The template image is used to reassemble the RAM disk with the proper headers and other data:

```
# rm -f ./stage1/018-3783-2.dmg
# xpwntool ./stage1-decrypted.dmg ./stage1/018-3783-2.dmg -t \
  ./firmware/018-3783-2.dmg -k encryption_key \
  -iv initialization_vector
```

Finally, you're ready to repack the firmware bundle. Jump into the *stage1* folder and use the zip tool to create the *stage1.ipsw* firmware bundle in your home directory:

```
# pushd stage1
# zip-r ~/stage1.ipsw .fseventsd *
# popd
```

Step 3: Use Xpwn to Customize the Stage 2 Firmware

The *stage1.ipsw* firmware bundle you created in step 2 created an "upgrade" image that will upgrade the system kernel (allowing self-signed binaries to run) while leaving the filesystem intact. We'll get to install it shortly, but first, you'll create a second stage firmware bundle that will install the forensic toolkit payload.

Ensure you still have root privileges. Create a new folder called *stage2* in the same location as the *stage1* and *firmware* folders, and copy the Pwnage firmware bundle into it:

```
# mkdir stage2
# cp ~/Desktop/iPhone1,2_2.0_5A347_Custom_Restore.ipsw .
```

Inside this folder, you'll see the same two files ending with a *.dmg* extension. The smaller of these files is the firmware's RAM disk. In this example, the file is named *018-3783-2.dmg*:

```
# ls -l stage2
drwx------  4 root  staff        136 Jun 25 23:23 .fseventsd
-rw-r--r--  1 root  staff  220221811 Jul 24 19:15 018-3782-2.dmg
-rw-r--r--  1 root  staff   26217752 Jul 26 00:57 018-3783-2.dmg
drwxr-xr-x  4 root  staff        136 Jun 25 23:29 Firmware
```

```
-rw-r--r--  1 root  staff      1668 Jun 26 00:09 Restore.plist
-rw-r--r--  1 root  staff   3863239 Jul 24 19:12 kernelcache.release.
s5l8900x
```

The RAM disk, being the same as before, will use the same encryption key and initialization vector as the stage-1 RAM disk. Use xpwntool, as shown here, to decrypt it into another file named *stage2.dmg*:

```
# xpwntool ./stage2/018-3783-2.dmg ./stage2-decrypted.dmg -k encryption_key \
  -iv initialization_vector
```

Once the operation completes, the newly created decrypted image will contain the raw HFS filesystem, which can be mounted in read-write mode. On Mac OS X, use the hdid tool, as shown below. On Windows, you'll need to use a tool like HFSExplorer:

```
# hdid -readwrite ./stage2-decrypted.dmg
```

The file will be mounted in */Volumes/ramdisk* on Leopard, just like the last archive, so be sure you've previously unmounted the stage 1 volume to avoid confusion. Once mounted, you'll need to delete some unneeded files to make room for the recovery payload. These were needed only by the first stage firmware bundle:

```
# rm -f /Volumes/ramdisk/usr/local/standalone/firmware/*
```

Some versions of firmware may require even more additional space be removed. If necessary, stage 2 packages may additionally delete the following files and directories from the RAM disk:

- */System/Library/Frameworks/Security.framework*
- */System/Library/Frameworks/CoreGraphics.framework*
- */System/Library/PrivateFrameworks/*.framework*
- */usr/sbin/asr*
- */usr/local/standalone/firmware/**
- */usr/local/bin/**

Now use the *stage2-prep.zip* archive from the downloadable examples web page to install the custom forensics payload and other tools. This will cause the firmware to skip the standard upgrade procedure and instead copy the forensic recovery toolkit to the device:

```
# unzip -od /Volumes/ramdisk /path/to/stage2-prep.zip
```

You must now manually edit the launch daemon property list, so that its local permissions will not be changed (using tar or zip appears to unavoidably change them, resulting in an inoperable RAM disk). Use a text editor such as vi and edit the file */Volumes/ramdisk/System/Library/LaunchDaemons/com.ap* *ple.restored_external.plist.* Under the `ProgramArguments` section, change the arguments to call the *install.sh* script using the `bash` interpreter, as shown below:

```
<key>ProgramArguments</key>
    <array>
        <string>/bin/bash</string>
        <string>/payloads/install.sh</string>
    </array>
```

Once complete, save the changes. When everything has been completed, the following files will have been changed or added to the RAM disk:

```
System/
System/Library/
System/Library/LaunchDaemons/
System/Library/LaunchDaemons/com.apple.restored_external.plist
bin/
bin/bash
bin/sh
bin/sync
payloads/
payloads/install.sh
payloads/openssh_4.7p1-5_iphoneos-arm.zip
payloads/openssl_0.9.8g-4_iphoneos-arm.zip
payloads/passwd.zip
payloads/recovery_toolkit.zip
sbin/
sbin/newfs_hfs
sbin/umount
usr/
usr/bin/
usr/bin/unzip
usr/lib/
usr/lib/libhistory.5.2.dylib
usr/lib/libhistory.5.dylib
usr/lib/libhistory.dylib
usr/lib/libicucore.dylib
usr/lib/libintl.8.0.2.dylib
usr/lib/libintl.8.dylib
usr/lib/libintl.dylib
usr/lib/libintl.la
usr/lib/libncurses++.a
usr/lib/libncurses++w.a
usr/lib/libncurses.5.dylib
usr/lib/libncurses.dylib
usr/lib/libncursesw.5.dylib
usr/lib/libncursesw.dylib
usr/lib/libreadline.5.2.dylib
usr/lib/libreadline.5.dylib
usr/lib/libreadline.dylib
usr/lib/libresolv.9.dylib
usr/lib/libresolv.dylib
usr/sbin/
```

```
usr/sbin/asr
usr/sbin/fdisk
```

Unmount the RAM disk. Use Xpwn to repack it into the correct format, and overwrite the original image:

```
# rm -f ./stage2/018-3783-2.dmg
# xpwntool ./stage2-decrypted.dmg ./stage2/018-3783-2.dmg \
  -t ./firmware/018-3783-2.dmg -k encryption_key \
  -iv initialization_vector
```

Finally, you're ready to rebuild the firmware bundle:

```
# pushd stage2
# zip -r ~/stage2.ipsw .fseventsd
# popd
```

Step 4: Install the Staged Firmware Bundles

You've now successfully created custom firmware bundles from Apple's iPhone software, and are ready to install them on the iPhone. Before installing the first bundle, you'll need to place the firmware into Device Failsafe Utility (DFU) mode. You did this in Pwnage to originally modify the boot ROM. The instructions are below:

1. Press and hold the Power button until prompted to "Slide to Power Off." Slide it to the right and ensure the device has completely powered itself down.

2. Press and briefly hold the Power button, then immediately release it after you see the device power on.

3. While the Apple logo is still displayed, press and hold the Power and Home buttons simultaneously until the device's power is forced off.

4. Wait five seconds. The screen will remain blank.

5. Release *only* the Power button, while still holding the Home button. The screen will remain blank.

6. Hold the Home button for another 10 seconds until iTunes recognizes "an iPhone in restore mode."

If you make a mistake at any time, you can simply power the device back down and try again.

The process to install the staging bundles, in order, is as follows:

1. After performing the steps above, ensure the iPhone is recognized in recovery mode.

2. Hold down the Option key (on Mac) or the Shift key (on Windows) and click Restore. You will be prompted with a file selection screen. Navigate to the *stage1.ipsw* file you created in your home directory and select it.

3. iTunes will upgrade the NOR to use a patched kernel cache prepared by Pwnage but should preserve your filesystem, as the destructive portions of the upgrade will fail gracefully. The process will look and feel like a standard restore.

4. Once the device has booted back into normal operating mode, cleanly power the device off using the "Slide to Power Off" mechanism. Once completely powered down, hold the Home and Power buttons for several seconds until the "Connect to iTunes" recovery screen appears.

5. iTunes will inform you that the device is in restore mode. Hold down the Option key (on Mac) or the Shift key (on Windows) and click Restore. You will be prompted with a file selection screen. Navigate to the *stage2.ipsw* file you created in your home directory and select it.

6. iTunes will attempt to perform a restore and complain that it has failed. This is normal. During this time, the iPhone will reboot. At this time, the OpenSSH daemon should be up and listening, the passcode removed, and the system password restored to `alpine`. You can SSH into it using the techniques described in the next chapter.

 If, at any time, the device appears to be stuck in recovery mode, place the device back into DFU mode and attempt to restore using the *stage2.ipsw* bundle.

The initial first stage restore processes must be performed in DFU mode, and not standard recovery mode. The second stage generally functions in recovery mode, but some problem devices may require DFU mode. If it becomes necessary to place the device into DFU mode, use the instructions outlined earlier for stage 1.

Removing the Forensic Recovery Toolkit

Later on, when you've finished examining the device, you'll want to remove the toolkit and undo any changes you've made. To do this, simply use the iTunes "Restore" mode function to restore the device to its original firmware. If data exists on the device, sync it first with a separate, protected user account on the machine to back up the data. You will then be able to restore this backup after the restore.

## CHAPTER 4

Forensic Recovery

In the previous chapter, you learned how to install a recovery toolkit on the iPhone. When the toolkit is installed, an OpenSSH daemon begins accepting connections on the device, and a Unix world is ready to service requests from the examiner. This chapter walks you through the process of configuring the iPhone to communicate with your desktop on the same Wi-Fi network so you can recover the raw media partition. Once recovered, you'll be introduced to data recovery tools for carving and validating files, which you'll use for further recovery of deleted files.

Configuring Wi-Fi and SSH

The media partition must be recovered over Wi-Fi, so your wireless network must be configured to connect the iPhone and desktop machine. Depending on the level of integrity your examination requires, the following options are available, each with differing levels of complexity:

- Use an insecure access point with or without an encrypted tunnel or MD5 digests
- Use a WPA-encrypted or WEP-encrypted access point
- Use an ad-hoc network

WEP-encrypted networks suffer from an initialization vector vulnerability, where a malicious actor could deduce the network key by watching encrypted traffic as it flows across the network. This means that a WEP-encrypted network is susceptible to potential tampering while your data is in transit. To counter this, you may choose to use a network supporting WPA (Wi-Fi Protected Access), which is newer and more secure. Alternatively, the md5 utility, installed with the recovery toolkit, can be used to create a cryptographic digest of the media partition before and after transmission to ensure that it has not been tampered with during transit.

Connecting to an Access Point

1. To configure wireless access on the iPhone, tap the Settings icon. A list of options will appear.

2. Tap the option labeled Wi-Fi, second down from the top. This will transition to a window where the wireless network can be configured. If Wi-Fi is turned off, tap the switch at the top to turn it on.

3. A list of available wireless networks will appear in the section labeled "Choose a Network Tap" on the network that your desktop is presently connected to. As the iPhone joins the network, a wait indicator will be displayed.

4. Once the network has been joined, tap the blue disclosure arrow to the right of the selected network. This will allow you to view and change the iPhone's IP address and other network settings.

5. Take note of the IP address of the iPhone, as you'll need it later. Use the ping utility on the desktop to ensure that the device is reachable. If it is not, one or both of the devices may be misconfigured, or the access point may enforce AP isolation.

 The procedure in this chapter will not work if your access point enables an "AP isolation" feature, which prevents devices on the network from communicating with other local devices. If your access point is configured in this fashion, you must either disable this feature or revert to using an ad-hoc network.

Creating an Ad-Hoc Network

If no access point is available, or if insecure devices are not permitted to connect to local access points by policy, the desktop can be configured to serve as its own access point. Both machines will require a static IP address.

Mac OS X

Leopard can easily create ad-hoc networks on the fly. To create an ad-hoc network:

1. Click on the AirPort icon located on the desktop's menu bar and select "Create Network..." from the menu.

2. You will be prompted to create a computer-to-computer network, and a new window will be presented that prompts you for information.

3. You may name the network anything you like—this example will use the network name forensics1.

4. Click OK to create the network and automatically join it.

At this point, your ad-hoc network has been created and your desktop is connected to it, but because your desktop doesn't run a DHCP server, a static IP address must be assigned. You can manually configure the wireless interface from a terminal window. Open the Terminal application in your Utilities folder and enter the following command to set the IP address of your wireless interface to 192.168.0.1:

```
$ sudo ifconfig en1 inet 192.168.0.1 netmask 255.255.255.0
```

 Certain versions of iPhone software appear to have difficulty connecting to an ad-hoc network that is encrypted. If you experience a problem joining the network, try recreating the network without a password.

Now connect your iPhone to the ad-hoc network:

1. Tap through Settings Wi-Fi.
2. You should see the name of your ad-hoc network on the network list (for example, forensics1). Tap the network and you should connect.
3. Once connected, configure the iPhone to have a static address on the network. Tap the blue disclosure arrow to bring up the iPhone's network settings.
4. Tap Static to set the information manually. Now enter an IP address of 192.168.0.2, a netmask of 255.255.255.0, and optionally the IP address of your ISP's DNS server.
5. Press the back button (labeled Wi-Fi Networks) for these changes to take effect.

You should now be able to ping the iPhone at IP address 192.168.0.2 from your desktop at IP address 192.168.0.1. If you can't, you've done something wrong, so go back and repeat these steps.

Windows

To create an ad-hoc network in Windows XP, perform these steps:

1. Open the control panel and choose Network Connections.
2. Right-click on your wireless connection and select Properties from the pop-up menu.
3. Click the Wireless Networks tab and click the Add button to add a new wireless network.

4. Enter the name of the network you would like to create. In this example, `forensics1` will be used.

5. Check the box titled "This is a computer-to-computer (ad hoc) network."

6. Once complete, click the Advanced tab and manually set the IP address of the wireless connection to 192.168.0.1 with a netmask of 255.255.255.0.

7. Save and apply all of your changes.

Your desktop machine will be automatically joined to the newly created network.

Now connect your iPhone to the ad-hoc network:

1. Tap through Settings Wi-Fi.

2. You should see the name of your ad-hoc network on the network list (for example, `forensics1`). Tap the network and you should connect.

3. Once connected, configure the iPhone to have a static address on the network. Tap the blue disclosure arrow to bring up the iPhone's network settings.

4. Tap Static to set the information manually. Now enter an IP address of 192.168.0.2, a netmask of 255.255.255.0, and optionally the IP address of your ISP's DNS server.

5. Press the back button (labeled Wi-Fi Networks) for these changes to take effect.

You should now be able to ping the iPhone at IP address 192.168.0.2 from your desktop at IP address 192.168.0.1. If you can't, you've done something wrong, so go back and repeat these steps.

SSH to the iPhone

Once the iPhone is active on the network, you connect to it via SSH from your desktop. If you have not already done so, install the SSH tools outlined in Chapter 2. Then enter the command:

```
$ ssh -l root x.x.x.x
```

 Replace *x.x.x.x* with the IP address of the iPhone. When prompted for a password, enter `alpine`, which is the root password set automatically when you install the forensics toolkit. If you are unable to connect, try pinging the device to ensure you have network connectivity.

Once you have successfully logged into the iPhone, you're ready to recover the media partition.

Recovering the Media Partition

With the recovery toolkit installed and the iPhone sharing a network connection with your desktop, the media partition can finally be recovered. Depending on what level of integrity you're looking to establish, there are many different ways to accomplish this. This section walks you through the different steps involved in recovering the media partition. Some processes are optional, and it will ultimately be up to you to determine which security options are important.

Prior to performing a recovery, it's a good idea to disable the iPhone's locking mechanism. Click on the Preferences icon, then General. Change the Auto-Lock option to Never.

Command-Line Terminal

Much of the work involved from here on out will be performed on the command line, so it's important to know how to invoke a command-line terminal window.

Mac OS X

Find the Terminal application by opening the Applications folder, and double-clicking on the Utilities folder. Double-click Terminal to open the application. Subsequent windows can be opened by selecting New Window from the Terminal menu.

Windows

Click on the Start menu, then highlight Programs, followed by Accessories. Click on the Command Prompt application. This will open a new window with what you may refer to as a "DOS prompt."

Tools Needed

To recover the media partition, you'll need two command-line tools on the desktop: dd and nc. The dd tool is a disk copy tool used to copy the raw drive image, while the nc tool (also known as netcat) is used to send (and receive) data across a network. Both of these tools must be installed on both the desktop and the iPhone. The recovery toolkit automatically installs the iPhone builds of these tools, leaving the desktop portion up to you.

The file copy over netcat is insecure unless forwarded through an SSH tunnel. In both cases, for evidentiary integrity, it is recommended that this copy be conducted over a private, encrypted wireless network, or that MD5 digests be used to verify the integrity of the image.

- Mac OS X Leopard includes these tools by default. To verify this, open a terminal and type **which dd nc**. Paths to both files should appear in the resulting output.

- Windows versions of these tools may be downloaded at *http://www.chrys ocome.net/dd* and *http://www.vulnwatch.org/netcat/*. An archive is also available on the O'Reilly website at *http://www.oreilly.com/ 9780596153588*.

MD5 Digests

Before transmitting the media partition to the desktop machine, it may be appropriate to generate an MD5 digest of it from the iPhone. This will ensure that the partition data hasn't been altered or tampered with while in transit. To do this, connect to the iPhone using SSH and issue the commands below into a terminal window, replacing *x.x.x.x* with the IP address of the iPhone:

```
$ ssh -l root x.x.x.x
# cd /
# umount -f /private/var
# mount -o ro /private/var
# md5 /dev/rdisk0s2
```

These commands connect to the iPhone via SSH and then change to the root (/) directory. Next, the umount command forcibly unmounts the */private/var* partition. Since other iPhone applications are using the disk, it cannot be unmounted without force (the -f option). Finally, the partition is remounted with the read-only option (ro) and the md5 tool is instructed to create a digest of its raw device.

In order to create a digest, the entire partition must be read and processed. Depending on the capacity of the iPhone, this may take several hours to complete. To keep the iPhone "alive" during this time, it may be necessary to occasionally swipe your finger across the screen in a way that won't activate any applications or user interface elements. If the iPhone falls asleep, it may shut down its wireless connection, which would cause the entire process to freeze. To keep the network connection alive, it's a good idea to run a ping session from the iPhone (in another terminal window) while waiting for the MD5 digest to return.

You can test the network connection by pressing Enter a few times in the terminal window. If you can see empty lines being echoed to your terminal window, the connection is still live.

While the user partition is mounted as read-only, the user interface (via the touch screen) *must not* be used, except to touch an inactive portion of the screen (to keep the backlight active). If, at any time, the operating system layer becomes nonresponsive, rebooting the device will cause the user partition to be remounted back in read-write mode. This will allow the operating system to write to the partition again, however, and so you'll need to reissue the commands above to generate another MD5 digest.

 To forcibly reboot the iPhone, hold the Home and Power buttons down only until the device powers off. Wait a few seconds and then hold down the Power button to power the device back on.

When completed, the md5 utility will return a digest of the raw disk partition, as shown below. Copy this output, after transferring the disk image across the network, as you will use it later to compare with a digest created on the desktop.

```
MD5 (/dev/rdisk0s2) = b5bd6ba33b37c45daf4e5cf520f48023
```

Unencrypted Recovery

The fastest and easiest way to recover the media partition is to send it directly to the desktop machine without any level of encryption. If you're using a WEP- or WPA-encrypted wireless network, the data will be encrypted on the network layer regardless. To send the disk partition, you'll need to run separate commands from both the desktop machine and the iPhone to transmit the disk contents across the network.

Your desktop and the iPhone are essentially going to play a game of catch. On the desktop side, you'll be issuing a command (using netcat) telling the desktop to listen on a network port. Think of a port like you'd think of third base —the desktop is being instructed to listen for incoming data at a certain location, and the iPhone is going to throw the ball (here, the disk image) to the desktop. Both have to be set up right, or the transmission will fail.

On the desktop side, instruct the netcat tool to listen on a local port (in this example, 7000). The information that the desktop receives is then sent to the disk copy utility, which is used to convert the data back into a disk image file.

Mac OS X

Issue the following from a terminal window:

```
$ nc -l 7000 | dd of=./rdisk0s2 bs=4096
```

Here's a breakdown of the command:

nc
> Calls netcat

-l
> Tells netcat to listen for incoming connections

7000
> Tells netcat to use port 7000

| dd
> Pipes (relays) the information received by netcat to the dd disk copy utility

of=./rdisk0s2
> Stores the disk image locally (of stands for "output file") with the filename *rdisk0s2*

bs=4096
> Uses a disk block size of 4 K

 Some versions of netcat for Mac OS X use the arguments -l -p 7000 instead of -l 7000.

Windows

Issue the following from a command prompt:

```
$ nc -L -p 7000 | dd of=./rdisk0s2 bs=4096
```

Here's a breakdown of the command:

nc
> Calls netcat

-L
> Tells netcat to listen for incoming connections

-p 7000
> Tells netcat to use port 7000

| dd
> Pipes (relays) the information received by netcat to the dd disk copy utility

`of=./rdisk0s2`

Store the disk image locally (`of` stands for "output file") with the filename *rdisk0s2*

`bs=4096`

Uses a disk block size of 4 K

Sending the data

After you tell the desktop machine to listen for incoming data, the terminal window on the desktop will appear to sit idle. This means it's waiting and listening for data. Open a second terminal window and connect to the iPhone using SSH. Use the following commands to instruct it to send its media partition to the desktop. In the sample commands, *x.x.x.x* represents the IP address of the iPhone, and *y.y.y.y* represents the IP address of the desktop machine:

```
$ ssh -1 root x.x.x.x
# /bin/dd if=/dev/rdisk0s2 bs=4096 | nc y.y.y.y 7000
```

Here's a breakdown of the send command:

`/bin/dd`

Calls the disk copy utility on the iPhone

`if=/dev/rdisk0s2`

Instructs disk copy to read the second partition of the raw disk as input

`bs=4096`

Uses a disk block size of 4 K

`| nc`

Pipes (relays) the information received by the disk copy utility to `netcat`

y.y.y.y

Since -1 wasn't specified, instructs `netcat` to send the data to (not receive from) the specified address

`7000`

Instructs `netcat` to use port 7000

The raw partition will begin transferring over the network, which should be reflected by a gradual increase in the size of the file on the local desktop. This operation may take several hours, depending on the capacity of the iPhone. Only the media portion of the iPhone's disk storage will be sent, so the actual file size will be less than the advertised capacity. When the file reaches its maximum size, you'll see both terminal windows report that a certain number of bytes have been sent or received. Once complete, it may be necessary to cancel the operation on the iPhone's side by pressing Ctrl-C.

If the operation fails prematurely, ensure that the iPhone is connected to the dock connector and is charging. The iPhone automatically shuts down its Wi-Fi when on battery as it enters sleep mode. If necessary, also set the Auto-Lock feature to Never in the iPhone's general settings to keep the display awake and unlocked. As a last resort, try running a ping from a separate terminal window on the iPhone, and occasionally swipe your finger across the screen to keep it from idling. If the operation persistently fails, check with your system administrator to ensure that it is not being hindered by firewall policies, and check the desktop machine to ensure its firewall is configured to allow access on the desired port (in this example, 7000).

Once complete, run the md5 command on your desktop machine to ensure the digest matches the one taken on the iPhone:

```
$ md5 rdisk0s2
MD5 (rdisk0s2) = b5bd6ba33b37c45daf4e5cf520f48023
```

The hexadecimal number following the equals sign should be exactly the same as the one you generated on the original image using the procedure described earlier in the section "MD5 Digests." If everything is fine, back up the disk image from the desktop and check it into a digital vault. All further file operations should be performed on a copy of the disk image.

Never try to examine an original disk image, only a copy. Some tools have been known to slightly alter the disk image in the course of their operation, thereby altering the digest. The disk image is also likely to be altered if mounted as a filesystem.

Now that the media partition has been copied, the iPhone itself may be analyzed by hand to obtain any information available through the standard user interface.

Encrypted Recovery of the Media Partition

Using a technique similar to the previous method, the disk image can be transmitted across an encrypted SSH tunnel, adding an extra layer of security (at the expense of added time) to your recovery efforts. This is done by creating a remotely forwarded network connection to the iPhone, so that all data transmitted across it will be encrypted by SSH. This helps prevent tampering and ensures that the data traveling across the wireless network is encrypted on an application layer. If you are using message digests or an encrypted access point, this step may be redundant.

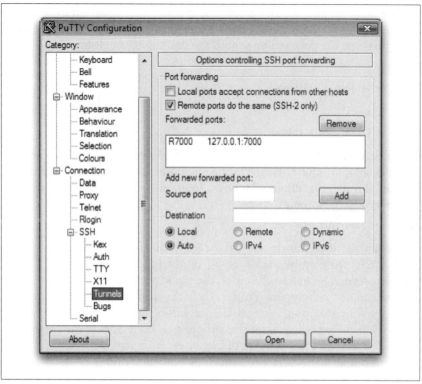

Figure 4-1. Remote port forwarding configuration in PuTTY

Along with the drawback of increasing transfer time, certain combinations of the SSH client and server can sometimes also result in packet size or other errors. In the event this occurs, you'll need to use a different SSH client on the desktop machine, or simply revert back to using the unencrypted technique described in the last section.

In the previous section, you connected to the iPhone using the simple SSH command:

```
$ ssh -l root x.x.x.x
```

To establish an encrypted tunnel, you'll need to spice this up a little. Add the following parameters to compress and remotely forward data:

```
$ ssh -l root -C -R 7000:127.0.0.1:7000 x.x.x.x
```

If you're using a GUI tool, such as PuTTY, instead of a command-line tool, configure a remotely forwarded port as shown in Figure 4-1.

On the desktop, instruct the `netcat` tool to listen on a local port as before (in this example, port 7000). There is no longer a need for the **dd** command, however. Just pipe the information sent to the desktop to the disk.

On Mac OS X:

```
$ nc -l 7000 > rdisk0s2
```

On Windows:

```
$ nc -L -p 7000 > rdisk0s2
```

On the iPhone, perform a raw partition dump. Instead of using the IP address of the desktop machine, use the localhost address of 127.0.0.1. This will feed the data through the iPhone's loopback interface, which will direct it through the encrypted SSH tunnel.

```
# cat /dev/rdisk0s2 | nc 127.0.0.1 7000
```

As the raw partition transfers across the SSH tunnel, activity should be reflected by an increase in the size of the file on the local desktop. This operation may take several hours, depending on the capacity of the iPhone, and will take longer than an unencrypted transfer. Only the media portion of the device's storage will be sent, so the actual file size will be less than the advertised capacity. When the file reaches its maximum size, both sides of the connection will report that a certain number of bytes have been sent (or received). When finished, it may be necessary to cancel the operation on the iPhone's side by pressing Ctrl-C.

 If the operation fails prematurely, ensure that the iPhone is connected to the dock connector and is charging. The iPhone automatically shuts down its Wi-Fi when on battery as it enters sleep mode. If necessary, also set the Auto-Lock feature to Never in the iPhone's general settings to keep the display awake and unlocked. As a last resort, try running a ping from a separate terminal window on the iPhone, and occasionally swipe your finger across the screen to keep it from idling. If the operation persistently fails, check with your system administrator to ensure that it is not being hindered by firewall policies, and check the desktop machine to ensure its firewall is configured to allow access on the desired port (in this example, 7000).

Once complete, run the `md5` command on your desktop machine to ensure the digest matches the one taken on the iPhone:

```
$ md5 rdisk0s2
MD5 (rdisk0s2) = b5bd6ba33b37c45daf4e5cf520f48023
```

The hexadecimal number following the equals sign should be exactly the same as the one you generated on the original image using the procedure described earlier in the section "MD5 Digests." If everything is fine, back up the disk image from the desktop and check it into a digital vault. All further file operations should be performed on a copy of the disk image.

 Never examine an original disk image, only a copy. Some tools have been known to slightly alter the disk image in the course of their operation, thereby altering the digest. The disk image is also likely to be altered if mounted as a filesystem.

Making Commercial Tools Compatible

Once a raw disk image has been recovered from the iPhone, it can be read by many commercial forensics tools such as Encase or FTK, but with one caveat. The disk image itself is reported as an HFS/X image (fifth generation HFS), which most tools do not yet recognize. The identifier for this format is located at or around offset 0x400 inside the image file. Changing the identifier from HX to H+ (denoting an HFS/+ filesystem) causes most existing tools to accept the file for processing. To make this change, document it and then use a hex editor, such as Hex Fiend or HexEdit 32. Figure 4-2 shows a segment of the file where the HX appears.

Data Carving Using Foremost/Scalpel

To recover deleted files, you need a data-carving tool. Data carving is the process of extracting structured data from unstructured data. Until mounted as a filesystem, the raw partition recovered from the iPhone looks like one big file to the computer, and contains both live and deleted data. A data-carving tool can scan the disk image for traces of desired files, such as images, voicemail, and other files. It then carves these smaller files out of the image for further analysis. Foremost and Scalpel are both data-carving tools.

Foremost is a free forensics tool developed by Special Agents Kris Kendall and Jesse Kornblum of the U.S. Air Force Office of Special Investigations. Foremost can be freely downloaded from *http://foremost.sourceforge.net* and compiled/ installed on most desktop operating systems. Mac OS systems may either build from sources or install using MacPorts (*http://www.macports.org*):

```
$ sudo port install foremost
```

Scalpel is a tool based on Foremost and performs much faster analysis using an identical configuration file. Scalpel is available at *http://www.digitalforen sicssolutions.com/Scalpel/*. Windows binaries for Scalpel are included in the

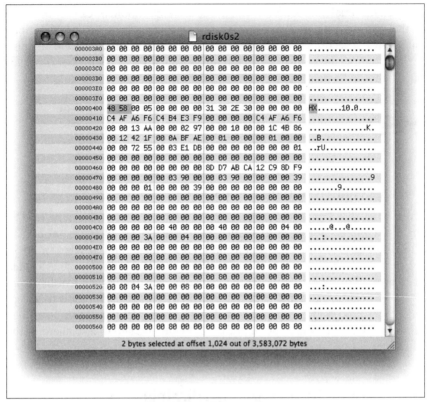

```
000003A0 00 00 00 00 00 00 00 00 00 00 00 00 00 00 00 00  ................
000003B0 00 00 00 00 00 00 00 00 00 00 00 00 00 00 00 00  ................
000003C0 00 00 00 00 00 00 00 00 00 00 00 00 00 00 00 00  ................
000003D0 00 00 00 00 00 00 00 00 00 00 00 00 00 00 00 00  ................
000003E0 00 00 00 00 00 00 00 00 00 00 00 00 00 00 00 00  ................
000003F0 00 00 00 00 00 00 00 00 00 00 00 00 00 00 00 00  ................
00000400 48 58 00 05 00 00 00 00 31 30 2E 30 00 00 00 00  HX......10.0....
00000410 C4 AF A6 F6 C4 B4 E3 F9 00 00 00 00 C4 AF A6 F6  ................
00000420 00 00 13 AA 00 00 02 97 00 00 10 00 00 1C 4B 86  ..............K.
00000430 00 12 42 1F 00 0A BF AE 00 01 00 00 00 01 00 00  ..B.............
00000440 00 00 72 55 00 03 E1 DB 00 00 00 00 00 00 00 01  ..rU............
00000450 00 00 00 00 00 00 00 00 00 00 00 00 00 00 00 00  ................
00000460 00 00 00 00 00 00 00 00 8D D7 AB CA 12 C9 8D F9  ................
00000470 00 00 00 00 00 03 90 00 00 03 90 00 00 00 00 39  ...............9
00000480 00 00 00 01 00 00 00 39 00 00 00 00 00 00 00 00  .......9........
00000490 00 00 00 00 00 00 00 00 00 00 00 00 00 00 00 00  ................
000004A0 00 00 00 00 00 00 00 00 00 00 00 00 00 00 00 00  ................
000004B0 00 00 00 00 00 00 00 00 00 00 00 00 00 00 00 00  ................
000004C0 00 00 00 00 00 40 00 00 00 40 00 00 00 00 04 00  .....@...@......
000004D0 00 00 00 3A 00 00 04 00 00 00 00 00 00 00 00 00  ...:............
000004E0 00 00 00 00 00 00 00 00 00 00 00 00 00 00 00 00  ................
000004F0 00 00 00 00 00 00 00 00 00 00 00 00 00 00 00 00  ................
00000500 00 00 00 00 00 00 00 00 00 00 00 00 00 00 00 00  ................
00000510 00 00 00 00 00 00 00 00 00 00 00 00 00 00 08 00  ................
00000520 00 00 04 3A 00 00 08 00 00 00 00 00 00 00 00 00  ...:............
00000530 00 00 00 00 00 00 00 00 00 00 00 00 00 00 00 00  ................
00000540 00 00 00 00 00 00 00 00 00 00 00 00 00 00 00 00  ................
00000550 00 00 00 00 00 00 00 00 00 00 00 00 00 00 00 00  ................
00000560 00 00 00 00 00 80 00 00 00 80 00 00 00 00 08 00  ................
```

2 bytes selected at offset 1,024 out of 3,583,072 bytes

Figure 4-2. Hex Fiend for Mac displaying offset 0x400

distribution. Scalpel can be compiled and installed on a Mac desktop using the following commands (if the version number has changed, simply substitute the current version in the following file and directory names):

```
$ tar -zxvf scalpel-1.60.tar.gz
$ cd scalpel-1.60
$ make bsd
$ sudo mkdir -p /usr/local/bin /usr/local/etc
$ sudo cp -p scalpel /usr/local/bin
$ sudo cp -p scalpel.conf /usr/local/etc
```

 To compile software on a Mac, Xcode Tools must be installed. This package can be downloaded free from the Apple Developer Connection website at *http://developer.apple.com*.

Data carving is by no means an exact technique, and some deleted data may be partially overwritten. Foremost and Scalpel both rise to the challenge by allowing examiners to specify headers (and optionally footers) that identify the beginning and end of the desired data they are searching for. The default configuration file includes data types for several different file formats, leaving it up to the examiner to uncomment the lines for files they want to carve out.

The format of the Foremost and Scalpel configuration files is identical, and equally simple to understand. A single entry consists of five fields: file extension, case sensitivity, default size, header, and optional footer:

```
jpg        y       200000  \xff\xd8\xff\xe0\x00\x10        \xff\xd9
```

In this example of a JPEG image, the extension is declared as *.jpg* and the pattern is identified as case-sensitive (the y in the second field). The default file size, which is used when the footer is either not specified or not found, is defined as 200 K. The header and footer are specified in hexadecimal by using the \x prefix, but plain text may also be used, as you'll see in the next section. In the previous example, the byte pattern FFD9 marks the end of this particular JPEG format. When the file is found, the data-carving tool will scan it until reaching the 200 K limit or finding the 0xFFD9 pattern. No more than 200 kilobytes will be stored in any one file that matched this configuration line. But most images, databases, and other files can still be used even if they contain extra junk at the end of the file. If files become truncated, you can increase the file size to get a larger chunk of data.

Configuration for iPhone Recovery

The Foremost tool uses a *foremost.conf* file for its configuration, while Scalpel uses an identical configuration, traditionally named *scalpel.conf*. Both sample configurations allow the examiner to uncomment certain types of files to be carved. Additional types may also be defined in the configuration, which you will sometimes find useful because the iPhone stores many proprietary files of interest that aren't represented in the Foremost and Scalpel configuration files. Edit the default configuration included with the software and uncomment any desired file types. Next, add the definitions that you find useful in the following sections.

Dynamic dictionaries

```
dat        y       16384   DynamicDictionary
```

Dynamic dictionary files are keyboard caches used by the iPhone to learn its owner's particular dictionary. Whenever a user enters text—whether usernames, certain passwords, website URLs, chat messages, email messages, or other form of input—much of it is stored (in order) in the keyboard cache. Adding the line shown here to the configuration file will search for deleted

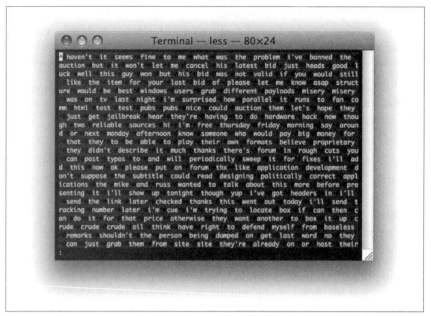

Figure 4-3. A deleted, two-week-old dynamic keyboard cache

and/or existing keyboard caches, revealing fragments of historical communication. An example of such a file is shown in Figure 4-3, containing fragments from multiple email messages, search engine lookups, and other user input.

Voicemail messages

```
amr        y      65535      #!AMR
```

The AMR codec is considered the standard speech codec by 3GPP, a collaborative standards body involved in mobile communications. It yields high-quality audio playback for voice content, and is used on the iPhone to store voicemail messages. Most voicemail messages fit nicely into 65 K, but to extract larger chunks of voicemail messages, simply increase the file size specified in the third field of this entry.

Property lists

```
plist      y      4096       <plist </plist>
```

A property list is an XML-like configuration file used heavily in the Mac OS world, including the iPhone. Many preloaded applications, as well as Apple's operating system components, use property lists to store anything from basic configuration data to history and cache information. By analyzing these files, the examiner can get an idea of what websites the suspect may have visited or what Google Maps direction lookups were queried. Other useful information may include mail server information, iTunes account info, and so on. The different property lists on the iPhone will be explained in the next chapter.

SQLite databases

```
sqlitedb    y    5000000   SQLite\x20format
```

The SQLite database format is widely used in the Mac OS X world to store calendars, address books, Google Maps tile graphics, and other information on the iPhone. SQLite databases are generally "live" on the filesystem, but older, deleted databases may be recovered in the event that the device was recently restored. Instructions for querying SQLite databases and recovering Google Maps tile graphics are covered in the next chapter.

Email

```
email      y    40960     From:
```

Scanning for email headers is an effective way to recover both live and deleted email.

Web pages

```
htm        n    50000     <html  </html>
```

Other files

```
pdf        y    5000000   %PDF-  %EOF
doc        y    12500000  \xd0\xcf\x11\xe0\xa1\xb1
```

Adobe PDF and Microsoft Word files can be stored locally when sent to the iPhone via email or navigated to using the iPhone's Safari web browser.

PGP blocks

```
txt        y    100000    -----BEGIN
```

PGP-encrypted messages are generally not of great use without a key, but can frequently include unencrypted messages within the same thread, should any have been sent/received.

Images

GIF, JPG, and PNG image formats are all used on the iPhone, and can be enabled for scanning by removing the comments preceding the corresponding lines in the configuration file. In addition to the default formats included, the following formats are used for various graphics on the iPhone.

```
png        y    40960     \x89PNG
```

This particular format of PNG is used to store small icons and Google Maps tile graphics.

```
jpg          y       5000000   \xff\xd8\xff\xe1      \x7f\xff\xd9
```

This is the JPEG format used for photos taken with the built-in camera.

 Be sure to enable the stock graphics formats in addition to the ones in this section.

Building Rules

If you're trying to recover a file that isn't listed in the above examples, you'll need to build your own rule to carve it out. Some methods for doing this are:

1. Identify the file format you're looking for. Many online resources can provide you with information for a host of different file formats.

2. Assemble a list of possible file headers. Use what information you can find about the file format to assemble a list of file headers that could have been used in the file you're searching for. Remember, it's better to generate too much data than not enough, so be liberal with your list—**grep** and other tools can help you sort through it.

3. Recreate the file structure using the same software or equipment, if possible. If you're trying to recover a file created with a particular software package, use that same software package to write a new file. In most cases, the first few bytes of the file header will be the same regardless of the file's contents. If you're trying to track down a file saved by a digital camera, video recorder, or other equipment, reproduce the steps to create another similar file, and examine its header.

Scanning with Foremost/Scalpel

Once a valid configuration file has been created, Foremost/Scalpel can be instructed to scan the image from the command line:

```
$ foremost -c foremost.conf rdisk0s2
foremost version 0.69
Written by Kris Kendall and Jesse Kornblum.
Opening /usr/local/sandbox /rdisk0s2
rdisk0s2:   0.9% |                        |   130.0 MB    11:07 ETA
```

If using Scalpel, replace the name of the application:

```
$ scalpel -c scalpel.conf rdisk0s2
```

Sometimes Scalpel tries to bite off more than it can chew in terms of system resources. If errors concerning the maximum number of file descriptors, or similar resource errors, are reported it may be necessary to run the tool with superuser privileges and use the `ulimit` command to lift resource restrictions. You're likely to run into this problem only when using Scalpel on Mac OS X:

```
$ sudo -s
$ ulimit && ulimit -n 8192
$ scalpel -c scalpel.conf rdisk0s2
```

The entire process may take a few hours to complete using Foremost, or less than a half hour using Scalpel. Potentially useful information will be recovered to a directory named *foremost-output* (or *scalpel-output*) within the current working directory. The tool will also create an *audit.txt* file within the output directory containing a manifest of the information recovered. Once recovered, it's up to the examiner to determine what data is valid.

Validating Images with ImageMagick

Recovery tools generally err on the side of generating too much data, rather than skipping files that could be important. As a result, they extract a lot of data that may be partially corrupt or unwanted altogether. Finding valid images to examine can be a time-consuming process in the presence of thousands of files, so a few simple recipes can greatly help reduce the amount of time needed.

The ImageMagick package contains a set of image processing utilities, one of which can be used to display information about images. The `identify` tool included with ImageMagick is perfect for sifting through the thousands of files created by data-carving tools to identify the readable images. ImageMagick can be downloaded from *http://www.imagemagick.org/script/index.php*. Mac OS users may build from sources or use MacPorts (*http://www.macports.org*) to install the package:

```
$ sudo port install imagemagick
```

Once installed, write a simple bash script to test the validity of an image file. For the purposes of this example, name the file *test-script.sh*:

```
#!/bin/bash
mkdir invalid
identify $1 || mv $1 ./invalid/
```

 Some images may be corrupt, but still somewhat recognizable. These images may appear invalid to the `identify` tool. It is therefore recommended that images only be moved, not deleted, so that invalid images can be later reviewed by hand.

When calling ImageMagick's `identify` tool for a given file, a successful exit code will be returned if the image can be read. The previous script moves all invalid images to a subdirectory named *invalid*, leaving the valid images in the original directory where you invoke the script. The script can then be invoked for a given supported image type (*.jpg*, *.gif*, *.png*, etc.) using a simple recipe with the `find` command:

```
$ mkdir invalid
$ chmod 755 test-script.sh
$ find foremost-output -type f -name "*.jpg" -exec ./test-script.sh {} \;
```

The syntax of the `find` command is subtle and replete with metacharacters. You can either stick to the script shown here and just adapt the *.jpg* file suffix, or explore the `find` documentation to discover its options for ownership, age of files, etc.

Strings Dump

As a final means to turn up data, the strings from the raw disk image can be extracted and saved to a file. The output will be enormous, but it will allow loose text searches for a particular conversation or other data.

Extracting Strings

To extract the strings from the disk image, perform the following.

Mac OS X

The `strings` utility comes integrated with Mac OS X, as it is a standard Unix tool. Simply issue the following from a terminal window:

```
$ strings rdisk0s2 > filename
```

Windows

Download the Windows version of `strings` from *http://technet.microsoft.com/en-us/sysinternals/bb897439.aspx*. Issue the following command to dump the text strings from the disk image:

```
$ strings.exe rdisk0s2 > filename
```

The Takeaway

- There are a lot of different security measures you can take to securely obtain the raw disk partition from the iPhone. Use the safest method that meets your goals. There is no need to overdo it.

- Data carving can be used to pull any type of data from a raw image or other file, but it's up to the examiner to have some clue about what to look for. If you're unsure, enable all file types and take the extra time to look through the results.

- Using simple tools like `strings` can give you a very large file of text to search through for key words or phrases.

## CHAPTER 5

Electronic Discovery

In the previous chapter, you learned how to recover the raw media partition from the iPhone and use data-carving tools to pull out potentially deleted images, email messages, and other useful files. This chapter will help you make sense of what you've recovered, and guide you through working with live data on the filesystem.

Data carving is very useful for recovering files that the suspect had intentionally deleted or forgotten about. The disk image can also be mounted as a live disk, allowing access to the live (not deleted) data on the iPhone. This allows you to examine the live filesystem and determine the data's filenames so that you know exactly what data is where.

 Instructions for working with the live filesystem commonly refer to the /mobile directory. If the iPhone is running firmware version 1.1.2 or earlier, these files are instead stored in /root. Be sure to make the necessary changes to your method to accommodate any changes in file location.

Converting Timestamps

Many of the timestamps found on the iPhone are presented in Unix timestamp format. To convert these to actual dates and times, use an online Unix timestamp converter, such as the ones found at *http://www.4webhelp.net/us/time stamp.php* and *http://www.onlineconversion.com/unix_time.htm*.

From the command line, a simple Perl script can be executed on Mac desktops:

```
$ perl -e 'require "ctime.pl"; print ctime(1200000000) . "\n";'
Thu Jan 10 16:20:00 2008
```

Mounting the Disk Image

When you transmit the disk image from an iPhone, you're getting a complete HFS/X filesystem (or HFS+ if you converted it). As a filesystem, this can be mounted on a Mac or Windows machine with a little work.

 Be sure you are working with a copy of the disk image by now, and not the original. The section "Unencrypted Recovery" in Chapter 4 explains why.

Disk Analysis Software

Before the disk image can be mounted, you may need to perform certain tasks or install software so that your computer can properly read the disk image.

Mac OS X and native HFS support

Mac OS X supports the HFS+ filesystem natively, so it is already able to read the disk image without any additional software. You'll need to rename the file you downloaded, however, to have a *.dmg* extension. You can then directly mount it from the finder:

```
$ mv rdiskOs2 rdiskOs2.dmg
$ hdid -readonly rdiskOs2.dmg
```

Once mounted, the volume should appear on the desktop and on the Finder's sidebar, listed under Devices. It can then be browsed to with the Finder or examined using Unix tools from a terminal window. The volume will be mounted in */Volumes*.

Windows and HFSExplorer

Windows doesn't understand the HFS/X disk image format by default, so you'll need a tool that's capable of reading the format. HFSExplorer is an application that can extract files from an HFS+ volume and load raw image files such as the one you dumped from the iPhone. It is published under the GNU General Public License (GPL) and is freely available at *http://hem.bredband.net/catacombae/hfsx.html*. To use HFSExplorer, you'll also need Sun's JVM (Java Virtual Machine) for Windows, also freely available at *http://www.java.com*.

1. Install HFSExplorer and Java for Windows.
2. Rename your disk image file to have a *.dmg* extension.
3. Start HFSExplorer.
4. Navigate to your disk image and click Open.

---

5. The volume should be visible in HFSExplorer, as shown in Figure 5-1.

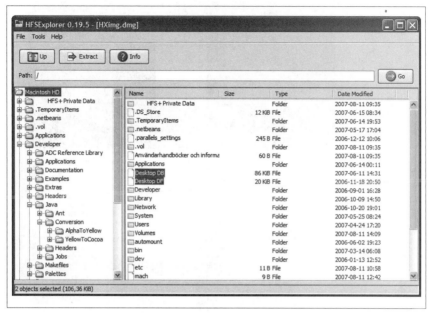

Figure 5-1. HFSExplorer for Windows

Graphical File Navigation

Both Mac OS X and Windows support preview panes within their file browsers. Mac OS X, in particular, provides a very useful graphical interface for browsing the directories and files created by the data carving described in Chapter 4.

Using Mac OS X, browse to the *scalpel-output* folder that is created during the data carving process (if you used the Scalpel tool). At the top of the finder window, a series of buttons should be visible, allowing you to select which view mode you'd like to use. Click the rightmost icon, which displays the cover flow view (Figure 5-2).

Figure 5-2. Cover flow view button

The contents of the directory will now appear in a graphical representation, including previews of images, HTML, and other readable files. The entire

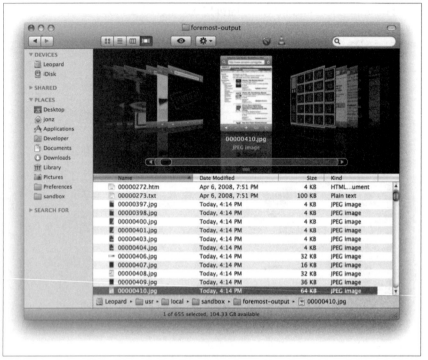

Figure 5-3. Cover flow view of recovered data (Mac OS X)

directory can now be visually examined, saving a considerable amount of time. See Figure 5-3 for an example of the display.

Many image files are likely to appear more than once, as they are sometimes rewritten when the iPhone syncs with a desktop. Album covers are also likely to appear several times, once for each song.

Images of Interest

Browsing through your recovered images directory may take some time, but can turn up both live and deleted files containing such valuable data as:

- Photos taken with the iPhone's camera
- Photos synced to the device from a desktop photo library
- Photos from the web browsing cache/history
- Google Maps tiles of maps or satellite imagery looked up by the suspect
- Multiple snapshots of running applications in the state they were in when the suspect pressed the home button, including:
  —Web browser "last page" visited (as shown in Figure 5-3)

—Contacts and dialer application screens

—Google Maps and YouTube "last viewed" screenshots

Many other images will also be recovered that are not necessarily useful, such as album covers (one cover per song), operating system images, and other stock graphics. Paths to "live" images of interest on the filesystem will be provided in the coming sections.

Extracting Image Geotags with Exifprobe

Geotagging is the process of embedding geographical metadata to a piece of media. In the iPhone's case, these are images. An iPhone running firmware v2.0 or greater can embed longitude and latitude coordinates inside images snapped with the built-in camera. Geotagging can be disabled when photos are taken, but in many cases, a suspect may either forget to disable it or fail to realize its consequences. By extracting the geotag from an image, you'll be able to pinpoint the general location where the photo was snapped.

As of firmware v2.0, geotag information is missing the degree of seconds, making an exact pinpoint impossible. This may be corrected in future versions.

Exifprobe is a camera image file utility developed by Duane Hesser. Among its features is the ability to extract image metadata. Download Exifprobe from *http://www.virtual-cafe.com/~dhh/tools.d/exifprobe.d/exifprobe.html*.

To check an image for geotags, call exifprobe on the command line:

```
% exifprobe -L filename.jpg
```

If the image was tagged, you'll see a GPS latitude and longitude reported, as shown below:

```
JPEG.APP1.Ifd0.Gps.LatitudeRef          = 'N'
JPEG.APP1.Ifd0.Gps.Latitude             = 42,57.45,0
JPEG.APP1.Ifd0.Gps.LongitudeRef         = 'W\000'
JPEG.APP1.Ifd0.Gps.Longitude            = 71,32.9,0
```

In this example, the photo was taken at 42.57450, –71.3290.

In addition to a geotag for the image, the timestamp that the actual photo was taken can be recovered:

```
JPEG.APP1.Ifd0.Exif.DateTimeOriginal    = '2008:07:26 22:07:35'
JPEG.APP1.Ifd0.Exif.DateTimeDigitized   = '2008:07:26 22:07:35'
```

SQLite Databases

The iPhone makes heavy use of database files to store information such as address book contacts, SMS messages, email messages, and other data of a personal nature. This is done using the SQLite database software (version 3), which is an open source, public domain database package. SQLite databases typically have the file extension *.sqlitedb*, but some databases on the iPhone have the *.db* extension instead. In order to access the data stored in these files, you'll need a tool that can read them. Good choices include:

- The SQLite command-line client, which can be downloaded at *http://www .sqlite.org*.
- SQLite Browser, a free, open source GUI tool for browsing SQLite databases. It is available at *http://sqlitebrowser.sourceforge.net*.

Mac OS X Leopard includes the SQLite command-line client, so we'll use command-line examples here. SQLite's command-line utility can easily access the individual files and issue SQL queries against a database.

 The basic commands you'll need to learn will be explained in this chapter. For additional information about Structured Query Language (SQL), read *Learning SQL* by Alan Beaulieu (O'Reilly).

Connecting to a Database

To open a SQLite database from the command line, invoke the `sqlite3` client. This will dump you to a SQL prompt where you can issue queries:

```
$ sqlite3 filename
SQLite version 3.4.0
Enter ".help" for instructions
sqlite>
```

You are now connected to the database file you've specified. To disconnect, use the .exit command; be sure to prefix the command with a period. The SQLite client will exit and you will be returned to a terminal prompt:

```
sqlite> .exit
$
```

SQLite Built-in Commands

After you connect to a database, there are a number of built-in SQLite commands you can issue to obtain information or change behavior. Some of the most commonly used commands are the following:

`.tables`

Lists all of the tables within a database. This is useful if you're not familiar with the database layout, or if you've recovered the file through data carving and are not sure which database you've connected to.

`.schema` *table-name*

Displays the SQL statement used to construct a table. This displays every column in the table and its data type. The following example queries the schema for the `mailboxes` table, which is found inside a database named `Envelope Index` on the iPhone. This database is used to store email on the device:

```
sqlite> .schema mailboxes
CREATE TABLE mailboxes (ROWID INTEGER PRIMARY KEY,
                        url UNIQUE,
                        total_count INTEGER DEFAULT 0,
                        unread_count INTEGER DEFAULT 0,
                        deleted_count INTEGER DEFAULT 0);
```

From this output you can learn that data in the table is indexed by an integer called `url` and that each item is associated with three other integer fields named `total_count`, `unread_count`, and `deleted_count`.

`.dump` *table-name*

Dumps the entire contents of a table into SQL statements. Binary data is output as long hexadecimal sequences, which can later be converted to individual bytes. You'll see how to do this later for recovering Google Maps cached tile images.

`.output` *filename*

Redirects output from subsequent commands so that it goes into a file on disk instead of the screen. This is useful when dumping data or selecting a large amount of data from a table.

`.headers on`

Turns display headers on so that the column title will be displayed whenever you issue a `SELECT` statement. This is helpful to recall the purpose of each field when exporting data into a spreadsheet or other format.

`.exit`

Disconnects from the database and exits the SQLite command shell.

Issuing SQL Queries

In addition to built-in commands, SQL queries can be issued to SQLite on the command line. According to the author's website, SQLite understands "most of the SQL language." Most of the databases you'll be examining contain only a small number of records, and so they are generally manageable enough to query using a simple SELECT * statement, which outputs all of the data contained in the table. Be sure to end the statement with a semicolon (;).

If the display headers are turned on prior to issuing the query, the first row of data returned will contain the individual column names. The following example queries the actual records from the `mailboxes` table, displaying the existence of an IMAP mailbox located at imap.domain.com (*http://imap.domain.com*). This mailbox contains 3 total messages, all of which have been read, and 0 deleted. The user's outbox shows that no messages are waiting to be sent:

```
sqlite> SELECT * FROM mailboxes;
1|imap://username@imap.domain.com/INBOX|3|0|0
2|local:///Outbox|0|0|0
```

Important Database Files

The following SQLite databases are present on the iPhone, and may be of interest depending on the needs of the case.

 These files exist on the media partition, which is mounted at */private/var* on the iPhone. The pathnames provided here are based on your local desktop mount of the disk image, and therefore will not include */private/var* in the path.

Address Book Contacts

The address book contains individual contact entries for all of the contacts stored on the iPhone. The address book database can be found at */mobile/Library/AddressBook/AddressBook.sqlitedb*. The following tables are primarily used:

ABPerson
> Contains the name, organization, department, and other general information about each contact.

ABRecent
> Contains a record of recent changes to properties in the contact database and a timestamp of when each was made.

ABMultiValue
> Contains multivalue data for each contact, including phone numbers, email addresses, website URLs, and other data for which the contact may have more than one. The table uses a `record_id` field to associate the contact information with a `rowid` from the ABPerson table. To query all of the

multivalue information for a particular contact, use two queries: one to find the contact you're looking for, and one to find their multivalue data:

```
sqlite> select ROWID, First Last, Organization, Department, JobTitle,
CreationDate, ModificationDate from ABPerson where First = 'Jonathan';
ROWID|Last|Organization|Department|JobTitle|CreationDate|
ModificationDate
22|Jonathan|O'Reilly Media|Books|Author|234046886|234046890

sqlite> select * from ABMultiValue where record_id = 22;
UID|record_id|property|identifier|label|value
57|22|4|0|7|jonathan@zdziarski.com
59|22|3|0|3|603-555-0000
60|22|3|1|7|603-555-0001
```

Notice the property field in the example. The property field identifies the kind of information being stored in the field. The most commonly used property codes are for email address (4), phone numbers (3), address (5), instant messenger account (13), and website URL (22).

Each record also consists of a label to identify how the data relates to the contact. For example, a phone number may be a work number, mobile number, etc. The label is a numerical value corresponding to the rowid field of the ABMultiValueLabel table, as shown by the first field on each line of output in the following example. Because rowid is a special column, it must be specifically named; the general SQL * would not return it:

```
sqlite> select rowid, * from ABMultiValueLabel;
rowid|value
1|_$!<Work>!$_
2|_$!<Main>!$_
3|_$!<Mobile>!$_
4|_$!<WorkFAX>!$_
5|_$!<HomePage>!$_
6|mobile
7|_$!<Home>!$_
8|_$!<Anniversary>!$_
9|other
10|work
```

ABMultiValueEntry

Some multivalue entries contain multiple values themselves. For example, an address consists of a city, state, zip code, and country code. For these fields, the individual values will be found in the ABMultiValueEntry table. This table consists of a parend_id field, which corresponds to the rowid of the ABMultiValue table.

Each record consists of a key/value pair, where the key is a numerical identifier describing the kind of information being stored. The individual keys are indexed starting at 1, based on the values stored in the ABMultiValueEntryKey table as shown below:

```
sqlite> select rowid, * from ABMultiValueEntryKey;
rowid|value
1|Street
2|State
3|ZIP
4|City
5|CountryCode
6|username
7|service
8|Country
```

Putting it all together

The query below can be used to cross-reference the data discussed in the previous sections by dumping every value that is related to any other value in another table (this dump is known in mathematics as a Cartesian product). This may be useful for exporting a suspect's contact information into a spreadsheet or other database. Use the following commands to dump the address book into a field-delimited text file named *AddressBook.txt*:

```
$ sqlite3 AddressBook.sqlitedb
SQLite version 3.4.0
Enter ".help" for instructions
sqlite> .headers on
sqlite> .output AddressBook.txt
sqlite> select Last, First, Middle, JobTitle, Department, Organization,
Birthday,
   ...>    CreationDate, ModificationDate, ABMultiValueLabel.value,
   ...>    ABMultiValueEntry.value, ABMultiValue.value
   ...> from ABPerson, ABMultiValue, ABMultiValueEntry, ABMultiValueLabel
   ...> where ABMultiValue.record_id = ABPerson.rowid
   ...>    and ABMultiValueLabel.rowid = ABMultiValue.label
   ...>    and ABMultiValueEntry.parent_id = ABMultiValue.rowid;
sqlite> .exit
```

Address Book Images

In addition to the address book's data, each contact may be associated with an image. This image is brought to the front of the screen whenever the suspect receives an incoming phone call from the contact. The address book images are stored in */mobile/Library/AddressBook/AddressBookImages.sqlitedb* and are keyed based on a record_id field corresponding to a rowid within the ABPerson table (inside the *AddressBook.sqlitedb* database). To extract the image data, first use SQLite's .dump command, as shown in the following example:

```
$ sqlite3 AddressBookImages.sqlitedb
SQLite version 3.4.0
Enter ".help" for instructions
sqlite> .output AddressBookImages.txt
```

```
sqlite> .dump ABImage
sqlite> .exit
```

This will create a text file containing the image data in a "binhex"-like encoding, reminiscent of the old TRS-80s and Apple][. In order to convert this output back into binary data, create a simple Perl script named *unbinhex.pl*, as follows.

 Perl is a popular scripting language known for its ability to easily parse data. It is included by default with Mac OS X Leopard. Windows users may download binaries and learn more about the Perl language at *http://www.perl.com*.

```perl
#!/usr/bin/perl

use strict;
use vars qw { $idx };

$idx = 0;
mkdir("./unbinhex-output", 0755);
while(<STDIN>) {
    chomp;
    unbinhex($idx, $_);
    $idx++;
}
exit(0);

sub unbinhex {
    my($idx, $data) = @_;
    my $j = 0;
    my $filename = "./unbinhex-output/$idx.png";
    next if int(length($data))<128;
    open(OUT, ">$filename") || die "$filename: $!";
    while($j < length($data)) {
        my $hex = "0x" . substr($data, $j, 2);
        print OUT chr(hex($hex));
        $j += 2;
    }
    close(OUT);
}
```

After saving this file, filter the contents of the *AddressBookImages.txt* file so that only the hexadecimal portions of the file remain. Each image should consist of a long string of hexadecimal characters, one line per image. The following command line filters the desired portions into a file named *Images.txt*:

```
$ grep ^INSERT AddressBookImages.txt | awk -F\' '{print $2}' > Images.txt
```

The contents of this file can now be fed directly into the Perl script:

```
$ cat Images.txt | perl unbinhex.pl
```

If you don't need an audit record of the image data extracted, you can simply pipe the output of the first statement directly into Perl, skipping the intermediate *Images.txt* file. The script will create a directory named *unbinhex-output*, containing a series of PNG images. These images can be viewed using a standard image viewer.

Google Maps Data

The Google Maps application allows iPhone users to look up directions or view a map or satellite imagery of a particular location. If the suspect performed lookups using this application, a cache of the most recently viewed titles may still be stored on the device. The database file */mobile/Library/Caches/Map Tiles/MapTiles.sqlitedb* contains image data of previously displayed map tiles. Each record contains an X,Y coordinate on a virtual plane at a given zoom level, and a binary data field containing the actual image data, stored in PNG-formatted images.

The Google Maps application also stores a cache of all lookups performed. The lookup cache is stored at the path */mobile/Library/Maps/History.plist* on the user partition, and can be easily read using a standard text editor. This lookup cache contains addresses, longitude and latitude, and other information about lookups performed.

Recovering the map tiles is a little trickier than retrieving the history, as the data resides in a SQLite database in the same fashion as the address book images. To extract the actual images, first copy the *MapTiles.sqlitedb* file onto the desktop machine and dump the `images` table using the command-line client, as follows. This will create a new file named *MapTiles.sql*, which will contain information about each map tile, including the raw image data:

```
$ sqlite3 MapTiles.sqlitedb
SQLite version 3.4.0
Enter ".help" for instructions
sqlite> .output MapTiles.sql
sqlite> .dump images
sqlite> .exit
```

Create a new file named *parse_maptiles.pl* containing the following Perl code. This code is very similar to the address book code used earlier, but it includes the X,Y coordinates and zoom level of each tile in the filename so that they can be pieced back together if necessary:

```
#!/usr/bin/perl

use strict;
use vars qw { $FILE };

$FILE = shift;
```

```
if ($FILE eq "") {
    die "Syntax: $0 [filename]\n";
}

&parse($FILE);

sub parse {
    my($FILE) = @_;
    open(FILE, "<$FILE") || die "$FILE: $!";
    mkdir("./maptiles-output", 0755);
    while(<FILE>) {
        chomp;
        my $j = 0;
        my $contents = $_;
        next unless ($contents =~ /^INSERT /);
        my ($junk, $sql, $junk) = split(/\(|\)/, $contents);
        my ($zoom, $x, $y, $flags, $length, $data) = split(/\,/, $sql);
        $data =~ s/^X'//;
        $data =~ s/'$//;
        my $filename = "./maptiles-output/$x,$y\@$zoom.png";
        next if int(length($data))<128;
        print $filename . "\n";
        open(OUT, ">$filename") || die "$filename: $!";
        print int(length($data)) . "\n";
        while($j < length($data)) {
            my $hex = "0x" . substr($data, $j, 2);
            print OUT chr(hex($hex));
            $j += 2;
        }
        close(OUT);
    }
    close(FILE);
}
```

If necessary, install Perl. Use the previous script to convert the SQL dump to a set of PNG images. These will be created in a directory named *maptiles-output* under the current working directory.

```
$ perl parse_maptiles.pl MapTiles.sql
```

Each map tile will be extracted and given the name *X,Y@Z.png*, denoting the X,Y position on a plane and the zoom level; each zoom level essentially constitutes a separate plane.

Calendar Events

The iPhone allows users to create calendar events and alarms, as well as to sync events with a desktop machine. To extract all of the suspect's calendar events, you'll want to look at */mobile/Library/Calendar/Calendar.sqlitedb*.

The most significant table in this database is the Event table. This contains a list of all recent and upcoming events and their descriptions:

```
$ sqlite3 Calendar.sqlitedb
SQLite version 3.4.0
Enter ".help" for instructions
sqlite> select * from Event;
ROWID|summary|location|description|start_date|start_tz|end_date|all_day|
calendar_id|orig_event_id|orig_start_date
36|Call into meeting|Boston Office|Meeting with sales|235074600|US/Eastern|
235078200|0|4|0|0
```

Each calendar event is given a unique identifier. Also stored is the event summary, location, description, and start/end times.

Unlike most timestamps used on the iPhone, which are standard Unix timestamps, the timestamp used here is an RFC 822 timestamp representing the date offset to 1977. To convert this date, determine the actual RFC 822 timestamp and add 31 years:

1. Enter the timestamp into the tool located at *http://www.silisoftware.com/tools/date.php* as a Unix timestamp.
2. Take the RFC 822 timestamp output and add 31 years.

Call History

One of the most useful databases on the iPhone is often the call history. The call history stores the phone numbers of the last people contacted by the suspect. As newer calls are made, the older phone numbers are deleted from the database, but often remain present in the file itself. Querying the database will provide the live call list, while performing a **strings** dump of the database may reveal additional phone numbers. This can be particularly useful if the suspect cleared the call log. The file */mobile/Library/CallHistory/call_history.db* contains the call history:

```
$ sqlite3 call_history.db
SQLite version 3.4.0
Enter ".help" for instructions
sqlite> .headers on
sqlite> select * from call;
ROWID|address|date|duration|flags|id
1|8005551212|1213024211|60|5|-1
```

Each record in the call table includes the phone number of the remote party, a Unix timestamp of when the call was initiated, the duration of the call in seconds (often rounded to the minute), and a flag identifying whether the call was an outgoing or incoming call. Outgoing calls will have the low-order bit of the **flags** set, while incoming calls will have it clear. Therefore, all odd-numbered flags identify outgoing calls and all even-numbered flags identify incoming calls.

In addition to a simple database dump, performing a `strings` dump of the file can recover previously deleted phone numbers, and possibly additional information.

```
$ strings call_history.db
```

Email Database

All mail stored locally on the iPhone (that is, mail that is not downloaded from an IMAP server) is stored in a SQLite database having the filename /mobile/Library/Mail/Envelope Index.

Unlike other databases, this particular file has no extension, but it is indeed a SQLite database. This file contains information about messages stored locally, including sent messages and the trash can. Data includes message headers, mailboxes, and the message data itself. This database is somewhat complex and contains six tables: `mailboxes`, `messages`, `message_data`, `properties`, `pop_uids`, and `threads`.

To obtain a list of mailboxes stored on the device, query the `mailboxes` table:

```
$ sqlite3 Envelope\ Index
SQLite version 3.4.0
Enter ".help" for instructions
sqlite> select * from mailboxes;
ROWID|url|total_count|unread_count|deleted_count
1|imap://suspect@imap.somedomain.dom/INBOX|1|0|0
```

From here, you'll learn what email accounts the suspect is using and can correlate this to the `mailbox` identifier for each message stored in the database:

```
sqlite> select rowid, sender, subject, _to, cc, date_sent, date_received,
mailbox, remote_mailbox, original_mailbox, read, deleted from messages;
ROWID|sender|subject|_to|cc|date_sent|date_received|mailbox|remote_mailbox|
original_mailbox|read|deleted
132|John Q. Public <johnq@public.dom>|Re: Your Order|suspect@somedomain.dom|
1212605129|1212605737|1|1|1|1|0
```

As you can see, the `messages` table shows you only the message headers. To extract the body of the message, query the `message_data` table, cross-referencing the `message_id` field with the `rowid` of the record, as shown here:

```
sqlite> select * from message_data where message_id = 132;
message_id|part|partial|complete|length|data
132|1||1|8400|Here are your order details... [rest of message]
```

To dump the entire message database into single records, these two queries can be combined to create a single joined query:

```
sqlite> select rowid, sender, subject, _to, cc, date_sent, date_received,
mailbox, remote_mailbox, original_mailbox, read, deleted,
```

```
data from messages, message_data
where message_data.message_id = messages.rowid;
```

 The email database is another good candidate for string dumping, as deleted records are not immediately purged from the file.

Notes

The notes database is located at */mobile/Library/Notes/notes.db* and contains the notes stored for the iPhone's built-in Notes application. It's one of the simplest applications on the iPhone, and therefore has one of the simplest databases. Notes are directly accessible through the device's GUI, but can also be queried using a SQLite client:

```
$ sqlite3 notes.db
SQLite version 3.4.0
Enter ".help" for instructions
sqlite> select creation_date, title, summary, data from Note,
note_bodies where note_bodies.note_id = Note.rowid;
creation_date|title|summary|data
235075039|Foo||Foo
```

In some cases, deleted notes can be recovered by performing a **strings** dump of this database. Performing a **strings** dump is just as straightforward:

```
$ strings notes.db
```

SMS Messages

The SMS message database contains information about SMS messages sent and received on the device. This includes the phone number of the remote party, timestamp, actual text, and various carrier information. The file can be found on the iPhone's media partition in */mobile/Library/SMS/sms.db*:

```
$ sqlite3 sms.db
SQLite version 3.4.0
Enter ".help" for instructions
sqlite> .headers on
sqlite> select * from message;
ROWID|address|date|text|flags|replace|svc_center|group_id|association_id|
height|UIFlags|version
6|2125551234|1213382708|Wanna go out tonight?|3|0||3|1213382708|38|0|0
```

Like the call history database, the SMS database also has a **flags** field, identifying whether the message was sent or received. The value of the low-order bit determines which direction the message was going. Messages that were sent will have this bit set, meaning the `flags` value will be odd. If the message was received, the bit will be clear, meaning the `flags` value will be even.

The SMS messages database is also a great candidate for a `strings` dump, to recover deleted records that haven't been purged from the file. An example follows of an SMS message that had been deleted for several days, but was still found in the SMS database:

```
$ strings sms.db
12125551234HPs
Hey. Is your iPhone book in any bookstores? Like Barnes & Noble?
```

Voicemail

The voicemail database contains information about each voicemail stored on the device, and includes the sender's phone number and callback number, the timestamp, the message duration, the expiration date of the message, and the timestamp (if any) denoting when the message was moved to the trash. The voicemail database is located in */mobile/Library/Voicemail/voicemail.db*, while the voicemail recordings themselves are stored as AMR codec audio files in the directory */mobile/Library/Voicemail/*.

```
$ sqlite3 voicemail.db
SQLite version 3.4.0
Enter ".help" for instructions
sqlite> .headers on
sqlite> select * from voicemail;
ROWID|remote_uid|date|token|sender|callback_num|duration|expiration|
trashed_date|flags 1|100067|1213137634|Complete|2125551234|2125551234|
14|1215731046|234879555|11
sqlite>
```

The audio files themselves can be played by any media player supporting the AMR codec. The most commonly used players include Quicktime and VLC.

Property Lists

Property lists are XML manifests used to describe various configurations, states, and other stored information. Property lists can be formatted in either ASCII or binary format. When formatted for ASCII, a file can be easily read using any standard text editor.

Binary Property Lists

When formatted for binary, a property list file must be opened by an application capable of reading or converting the format to ASCII.

Mac OS X

Mac OS X includes a tool named Property List Editor. This can be launched by simply double-clicking on a file ending with a *.plist* extension.

Windows

Two tools can help you view binary property lists:

*   An online tool at *http://140.124.181.188/~khchung/cgi-bin/plutil.cgi* can convert property lists to ASCII format. The website is a simple wrapper for an online conversion script hosted at *http://homer.informatics.indiana .edu/cgi-bin/plutil/plutil.cgi/*.
*   Source code for an open source property list converter is available on Apple's website at *http://www.opensource.apple.com/darwinsource/10.4/ CF-368/Parsing.subproj/CFBinaryPList.c*. You'll have to compile and install the application yourself, and an Apple developer account is required. However, registration is free of charge.

Important Property List Files

The following property lists are stored on the iPhone and may contain useful information:

/mobile/Library/Cookies/Cookies.plist
> Contains website cookies saved from the Safari web browser. These can be a good indication of what websites the user has been actively visiting, and whether he has an account on the site.

/mobile/Library/Mail/Accounts.plist
> [Binary Format]
>
> Contains a list of email server accounts configured on the device, and pathnames on the media partition where remotely downloaded email is stored. You can open these paths to recover plain text files containing IMAP email and other remotely stored email.

/mobile/Library/Maps/History.plist
> Contains the Google Maps history. This is in XML format and includes the addresses of any direction lookups, longitude and latitude, query name (if specified), the zoom level, and the name of the city or province where the query was made. Example 5-1 shows a sample of the format.

Example 5-1. Cached map lookup for Stachey's Pizzeria in Salem, NH

```
<!DOCTYPE plist PUBLIC "-//Apple Computer//DTD PLIST 1.0//EN"
"http://www.apple.com/DTDs/PropertyList-1.0.dtd">
<plist version="1.0">
```

```xml
    <dict>
        <key>HistoryItems</key>
        <array>
            <dict>
                <key>EndAddress</key>
                <string>517 S Broadway # 5 Salem NH 03079</string>
                <key>EndAddressType</key>
                <integer>0</integer>
                <key>EndLatitude</key>
                <real>42.753463745117188</real>
                <key>EndLongitude</key>
                <real>-71.209228515625</real>
                <key>HistoryItemType</key>
                <integer>1</integer>
                <key>StartAddress</key>
                <string>Bracken Cir</string>
                <key>StartAddressType</key>
                <integer>2</integer>
                <key>StartLatitude</key>
                <real>42.911163330078125</real>
                <key>StartLongitude</key>
                <real>-71.570281982421875</real>
            </dict>
            <dict>
                <key>HistoryItemType</key>
                <integer>0</integer>
                <key>Latitude</key>
                <real>32.952716827392578</real>
                <key>LatitudeSpan</key>
                <real>0.023372650146484375</real>
                <key>Location</key>
                <string>Salem</string>
                <key>Longitude</key>
                <real>-71.477653503417969</real>
                <key>LongitudeSpan</key>
                <real>0.0274658203125</real>
                <key>Query</key>
                <string>Stachey's</string>
                <key>SearchKind</key>
                <integer>2</integer>
                <key>ZoomLevel</key>
                <integer>15</integer>
            </dict>
        </array>
    </dict>
```

</plist>, */mobile/Library/Preferences*

Various property lists containing configuration information for each application and service on the iPhone. If third-party applications have been installed on the device, they will also store their own configuration files here.

/mobile/Library/Safari/Bookmarks.plist

[Binary Format]

Safari browser bookmarks saved on the device. These may have been set directly through the device's GUI, or represent copies of the bookmarks stored on the suspect's desktop machine.

/mobile/Library/Safari/Bookmarks.plist.anchor.plist

[Binary Format]

The timestamp identifying the last time Safari bookmarks were modified.

/mobile/Library/Safari/History.plist

[Binary Format]

Contains the Safari web browser history since it was last cleared.

/mobile/Library/Safari/SuspendState.plist

[Binary Format]

Contains the last state of the web browser, as of the last time the user pressed the Home button, powered off the iPhone, or the browser crashed. This contains a list of windows and websites that were open so that the device can reopen them when the browser resumes, and represents a snapshot of the last web pages looked at by the suspect.

/root/Library/Lockdown/data_ark.plist

Stored in the root user's library, this file contains various information about the device and its account holder. This includes the owner's Apple Store ID, specified with `com.apple.mobile.iTunes.store-AppleID` and `com.apple.mobile.iTunes.store-UserName`, time zone information, SIM status, the device name as it appears in iTunes, and the firmware revision. This file can be useful when trying to identify external accounts belonging to the suspect.

/root/Library/Lockdown/pair_records

This directory contains property lists with private keys used for pairing the device to a desktop machine. These records can be used to prove that a specific desktop machine was paired and synced with the device at a given time. Certificates from this file will match certificates located on the desktop machine in one of the property lists located in */Users/username/ Library/Lockdown* (Mac OS X) or :*\Documents and Settings\username\Lo cal Settings\Application Data\Apple Computer\Lockdown* (Windows). See Chapter 6 for more information about desktop traces.

Other Important Files

This section lists some other potentially valuable files that don't fall into a particular class. Although each case may call for different evidence, the files covered in this section are generally useful for most types of examination.

/mobile/Library/Keyboard/dynamic-text.dat
A binary keyboard cache containing text entered by the user.

 The text displayed may be out of order or consist of various "slices" of different threads assembled together. View it using a hex editor or a paging utility such as less.

/mobile/Library/Preferences/com.apple.Maps.plist
Contains the last longitude and latitude coordinates viewed in the Google Maps application.

/mobile/Library/Preferences/com.apple.Safari.plist
Contains a list of recent searches performed in Safari.

/mobile/Library/LockBackground.jpg
The current background wallpaper set for the device.

/mobile/Media/WebClips
Contains a list of web pages assigned as buttons on the device's home screen. Each page will be housed in a separate directory containing a property list named *Info.plist*. This property list contains the title and URL of each page.

/mobile/Media/DCIM/100APPLE
Photos taken with the device's built-in camera and accompanying thumbnails.

/mobile/Media/iTunes_Control/Music
Location of all music synced with the device.

/root/Library//Caches/locationd/cache.plist
Contains the last coordinates fixed on by the GPS (iPhone 3G only).

CHAPTER 6

Desktop Trace

Recovering evidence from an iPhone can be an important step in building evidence for a case, but you can also find a wealth of information on any desktop machines that have been previously synced with the device. In a criminal investigation, a search warrant can be obtained to seize desktop equipment belonging to the suspect. In a corporate investigation, company-owned desktop or notebook machines can usually be examined.

The evidence found on a desktop or notebook computer can provide information about the trusted pairing relationship to the iPhone. The computer can also store backup copies of various data files, which are useful if the iPhone has been damaged or destroyed. This information can be used both as evidence and to further prove a relationship between the desktop and mobile device. If the suspect is trying to claim that the iPhone in evidence doesn't belong to him, this is a great way to disprove it.

This book doesn't cover desktop forensics, but assumes that the reader is familiar with desktop procedures. Most of the information gathered on the desktop can be found on the live filesystem, unless it has been deleted. Nonetheless, you should have a firm understanding of the procedures necessary to preserve evidence on the desktop, or the information you obtain may not be admissible. For more information about desktop forensics, check out *File System Forensic Analysis* by Brian Carrier (Addison-Wesley Professional).

A desktop trace should be gathered through standard forensic recovery procedures on the desktop machine. Both live and deleted data can be of great use to the examiner. This chapter describes the types of relevant data present on the desktop.

Proving Trusted Pairing Relationships

"The phone's not mine," the suspect insists. "I took it off this dude who owed me money."

You reply, "Look, it's got your prints all over it. It's yours."

The suspect starts grinning. "Prove it."

Cheesy dialogues like this often make their way into the latest TV shows, but there is a serious theme to all of this: when such a small device is seized, possession can often be confused with ownership. It's important to get rid of any reasonable doubt of the device's ownership before making a final case against the suspect.

Even though you found the iPhone on the suspect when you arrested him, it can sometimes be difficult to prove that the device really does belong to him. In the case of a drug dealer, the only real proof of ownership may be a few photos of a drug stash and some contacts who know him only by an alias. His contacts might be prepaid, or he may have used the last name "hoe" for all of his girlfriends, as one suspect did, so they can't be easily tracked down. His email account could even be Gmail, making it more ambiguous. You may know very well that the iPhone belongs to him, but if you can't prove it in court, any evidence might not be admissible. How can you prove that the phone (and the digital evidence on it) belongs to him?

To add more consideration for trusted pairing relationships, consider that the iPhone may not belong to the suspect, but rather was stolen from the victim. If the victim was killed in a robbery, his iPhone may have been wiped and is now being used by the suspect. Not only can you prove a trusted pairing relationship to the suspect's computer, but also to the victim's, definitively linking all three.

Every time the iPhone is synced with a desktop machine, it leaves behind trace evidence that can be used to link the two. If you can establish that the desktop machine in the suspect's house knows about the iPhone, you can demonstrate to a jury that the iPhone is tied to his personal user account. The iPhone and the desktop share a set of pairing records, which are essentially keys used for sharing data. Proving that the device was paired with a particular desktop machine can be of vital importance in a case like the one just discussed, especially if you can secure the suspect's desktop machine.

Pairing Records

In the last chapter, you learned about evidence discovery and all of the different files on the iPhone that contain useful information. In addition to these files, the directory */root/Library/Lockdown/pair_records* stores pairing records for all the desktop machines with which the iPhone has been paired. Certificates inside these pairing records are copied to any paired desktop machines, proving that the two were configured to exchange data at some point. The timestamps of the files on both devices can establish the date and time the most recent pairing took place.

If the device was paired with multiple machines, multiple pairing records will exist in the *pair_records* directory on the device. Take the following example. On one particular iPhone, a record exists in the pairing directory with the following filename, representing a unique identifier given to the desktop machine:

/var/root/Library/Lockdown/pair_records/38798B80-D800-4691-916A-01640D8CECCD.plist

 The identifier changes from desktop to desktop, so you'll need to obtain a file listing of the *pair_records* directory in order to know the exact filenames of the pairing records stored on the iPhone you are examining.

Inside the property list you will find the actual pairing certificate. The pairing record is stored in XML format. This particular iPhone contains the following device certificate:

```
<key>DeviceCertificate</key>
    <data>
    LSotLS1CRUdJTiBDRVJUSUZJQoFURSotLSotCk1JSUNOakNDQVI2ZOF3SUJBZOlCQURB
    TkJna3Foa2lHOXcwQkFRVUZBREFBTUIOWERUQTRNRFF3TORFek1qUXkKT1ZvWERURTRN
    RFF3TmpFek1qUXlOVm93QURRMm56QU5CZ2txaGtpRzl3MEJBUVGQUFPQmpRQXdnWWtD
    Z1lFQQp3djdjBzSDgycW9pcFM4Z2hZSnJPV1BLTOU3UUR5QmIxTkpuRmF2eDZEVVdwWWGEx
    NXhmN2JiN2VaVlAzaXZrGtUCkpBdOFPM1puTopGQTBFUzU4Nz1BTnVDM1R6cFpOT29S
    WFBhZWNlU3BmSG1RWEN6RUdCdUNDbOE5TmYwSWwxSjgKYUcxdnZPUjZTbWdFNE9ES2da
    by9UdGcybHIzTlRUSGlFbmVUWTJpSHp1OENBdOVBQWFNL01EMHdEQVlEVlIwVApBUUUgv
    QkFJdOFEQWRCZOSWSFEORUZnVUVUOdnpKcGpUMDloNEVPZHFuUi9mTjVmYVhVZDB3RGdZ
    RFZSMFBBUUgvCkJBUURBZ1dUUEwRONTcUdTSWIzRFFFQkJRVUFBNElCQVFCCa256SUZP
    ZFBYcUkrSGQOKzJNdDRjQTM2QWgwVDgKYONVVDJ2ZnF6WEIL3k2OFZFdnJkbU5zR1V5
    YmMwNOg4V21Ib1FtaDROMDFPdE5uNFpOUUdzK2k1QmxSRHRFcwpxUnJtanRndGFGGMkh2
    NFRpdGlBcWtsRX13cHY2azRLRFlRUkN5OTB1MCtQbTkwempzRy8zTzR5eHJhdk51YO5M
    CnFjalRGNOhHbmZ2Y2tGSVBYeG1SMlBhb2dySUxGLytpbDVGcThIVWx1dW5qbnAwbEz
    T31qQ29sbyt4c2NpeDgKZOFIU2pMDBvdU85cTVkSFc2cmRRRG1kaXlLbDRDUd1dOeDJH
    VEU4Sm1PZmRteFgwb21MQ2RXNWUyNOJGTHNnVgprZWh2bzZlWWlpuK3EyWU5NWDFkaTNt
    akx6aHFHRXRHRHUisxZk5RSUtDUWEzN3ptZY3lpWUtHeDFFmOAotLSotLUVORCBDRVJUSUZJ
    QoFURSotLSotCg==
    </data>
```

This certificate is base64 encoded. The decoded copy of the certificate looks like this:

```
-----BEGIN CERTIFICATE-----
MIICNjCCAR6gAwIBAgIBADANBgkqhkiG9w0BAQUFADAAMB4XDTA4MDQwODEzMjQy
NVoXDTE4MDQwNjEzMjQyNVowADCBnzANBgkqhkiG9w0BAQEFAAOBjQAwgYkCgYEA
wvOsH82qoipS8ghYJrOWPKOE7QDyBb1NJnFavx6DUWpXa15xf7bb7eZVP3ivkdkT
JAwAO3ZnOJFAOES5879ANuC3TzpZNOoRXPaeceSpfHmQXCzEGBuCCoA9NfOIl1J8
aG1vvOR6SmgE4ODKgZo/Ttg2lr3NTTHiEneTY2iHzu8CAwEAAaM/MDOwDAYDVROT
AQH/BAIwADAdBgNVHQ4EFgQU4vzJpjTO9h4EOdqnR/fN5faXUdowDgYDVROPAQH/
BAQDAgWgMAOGCSqGSIb3DQEBBQUAA4IBAQBknzIFOdPXqI+Hd4+2Mt4cA36AhoT8
cCUT2vfqzXLH/y68VEvrdmNsGUybcO7H8WiHoQmh4NO1OtNn4ZNQGs+i5BlRDtEs
qRrmjtMtaF2Hv4TitiAqklEywpv6k4KDYQRCy9OuO+Pm9OzjsG/3O4yxravNucNL
qcjTF7HGnfvckFIPXxiR2PaogrILF/+il5Fq8HUleunjnpOlIsOyjColo+xscix8
gAHSjIOoouO9q5dHW6rdQDiJiyKl4TwWNx2GTE8JmOfdmxXOomLCdW5e27BFLsgV
kehvo6eZZn+q2YNMX1di3mjLzhqGEtGR+1fNQIKCQa37zmcyiYKGx1f8
-----END CERTIFICATE-----
```

This same certificate will be found on the desktop machine to which this pairing record belongs. The filenames storing the information are symmetric: while the iPhone uses the desktop's unique identifier, the desktop stores the same certificate using the iPhone's unique identifier. For example, the certificate here was located in a property list named *d5d9f86cfc06f8bce3d31c551ccc69788c4579ea.plist* on the desktop machine. The filename refers to the unique identifier assigned to the iPhone device when it was activated.

See "Activation Records," later in this chapter, for more information on matching the unique device identifier itself.

The location of the pairing files stored on the desktop machine depend on the operating system:

Operating system	Location
Mac OS X	/Users/*username*/Library/Lockdown/
Windows XP	C:\Documents and Settings*username*\Local Settings\Application Data\Apple Computer\Lockdown
Windows Vista	C:\Users*username*\AppData\Roaming\Apple Computer\Lockdown

Newer versions of iTunes may change these locations.

Text comparison tools such as `diff` and `grep` can make matching up the certificates relatively effortless. Simply copy certificates from the iPhone and each desktop into separate files and perform a `diff` to determine whether the files differ, or `grep` through the files stored on the desktop machine using the encoded portions of the device certificate as match criteria.

Serial Number Records

In addition to pairing records, a manifest is written to the desktop machine to keep track of the names and serial numbers of devices paired with it, allowing the examiner to verify that a desktop not only knows how to sync with a particular iPhone, but also knows the iPhone's hardware serial number. The manifest file can be used to match the serial number recorded in the file with the serial number of the mobile device.

 The serial number of the mobile device can be obtained by tapping the Settings button on the device and then selecting General About.

Mac OS X

A binary property list with a filename beginning with *com.apple.iTunes* may be found in the directory */Users/username/Library/Preferences/ByHost*. Each host paired with the device will be assigned a separate file in this directory. The property list stores information about the device in a binary format, but you can use the `strings` tool described in earlier chapters to dump the ASCII data encapsulated within the binary information and search for the mobile device's serial number:

```
$ strings com.apple.iTunes.001b619668af.plist
```

Scan through the output of this command and visually search for the device's serial number, or use the `grep` command to scan for a specific string.

Windows XP

A match to the serial number can be found in a file named *C:\Documents and Settings\username\Local Settings\Application Data\Apple Computer\iTunes \iPodDevices.xml*.

Windows Vista

A match to the serial number can be found in a file named *C:\Users\username \AppData\Local\Apple Computer\iTunes\iPodDevices.XML*.

Device Backups

If the iPhone was damaged or destroyed, it may not be possible to get as much information off of it. This is when the device's backup files are of particular importance. Any time an iPhone is synced with a desktop machine, a backup of its configuration, address book, SMS database, camera photo cache, and other personal data is stored on the desktop in backup files. Each device paired with the desktop is assigned a special backup directory named after the device's unique identifier. Within this directory can be found a backup manifest, device information, and the individual data files. These files are normally copied back to the device in the event that the device is restored to its factory settings by the owner. While a suspect could manually delete such backups, many are not aware that such backups are being made, or choose to store the backups anyway.

 The serial number of the iPhone can also be found in device backup files on the desktop machine.

Device backups can be found in the following locations, depending on your operating system:

Operating system	Location
Mac OS X	/Users/*username*/Library/Application Support/MobileSync/Backup/*deviceid*
Windows XP	C:\Documents and Settings*username*\Application Files\MobileSync\Backup*deviceid*
Windows Vista	C:\Users*username*\AppData\Roaming\Apple Computer\MobileSync\Backup*deviceid*

The backup manifest file, *Info.plist*, contains a device profile including the serial number of the paired device, firmware revision, phone number, and timestamp. This can be used to prove not only that the two devices were paired, but also that a particular phone number was active when the device was synced. This can be useful if phone records are included as evidence in the investigation.

This backup directory will contain multiple files ending with a *.mdbackup* extension. Each file is a binary property list containing the filename and binary data for a single file backed up from the device. The binary data can be extracted by saving it as a text file using a property list editor (described in the previous chapter) or manual techniques.

To view the contents of a backup file, make a copy of it and rename the *.mdbackup* extension to *.plist*. This will allow the file to be opened with a

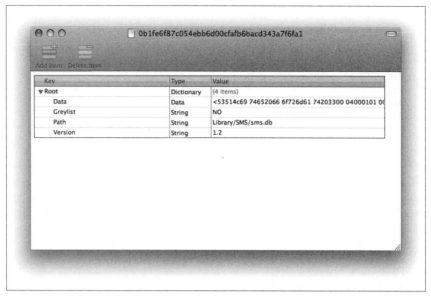

Key	Type	Value
▼ Root	Dictionary	(4 items)
Data	Data	<53514c69 74652066 6f726d61 74203300 04000101 00
Greylist	String	NO
Path	String	Library/SMS/sms.db
Version	String	1.2

Figure 6-1. Extracting a camera photo from a desktop backup file

property list editor. Inside the property list, the binary data for the file can be found and dumped. Once extracted, it can be analyzed using the techniques described in the previous chapter, depending on the type of file it is. See Figure 6-1.

The file type can be ascertained by looking at the filename given to the backup file in the Path section of the property list.

Activation Records

When an iPhone is activated, various information about the device is stored within the device's activation records. Activation records can be found on the iPhone in the directory */private/var/root/Library/Lockdown/activation_re cords*, which will be accessible as */root/Library/Lockdown/activation_records* on the user disk image. The information is stored using a base64 encoding and can be easily decoded back to plain text using any base64 decoder or the openssl command-line tool.

Inside the *activation_records* directory is a property list containing several different certificates. This includes the FairPlay certificate for encrypted music on the device and various account tokens. For an investigation, the most useful section is the AccountToken section of the property list:

```
<?xml version="1.0" encoding="UTF-8"?>
<!DOCTYPE plist PUBLIC "-//Apple Computer//DTD PLIST 1.0//EN"
"http://www.apple.com/DTDs/PropertyList-1.0.dtd">
<plist version="1.0">
<dict>
        <key>AccountToken</key>
        <data>
        ... data follows ...
```

When decoded, the information in this section contains the unique device identifier assigned when the pairing relationship to the desktop was made. This identifier will determine the filename of pairing records on the desktop machine. An activation ticket and hardware identities (including the IC Card, mobile subscriber, and mobile equipment identity) are also stored.

To decode the information in this section, paste the encoded portion of it into a separate file and use a base64 decoder, such as openssl:

```
$ openssl enc -d -base64 -infilename
{
    "ActivationRandomness" = "AEC80D06-1948-494C-846E-9A9FC02CF175";
    "UniqueDeviceID" = "d5d9f86cfc06f8bce3d31c551ccc69788c4579ea";
    "ActivationTicket" =
"0200000029338284e1a7309dd143c60aa20a7176fba9d1db44860ba2e8b214c471e3d06
b92089c06826dcc7a4f06e8200228d974cf6b5518baebe3457ccaffe9395a81d5a94a8e3
a7c1c71746aaebc39d9ddc3acf2fd359448dd2d2379782606a4eec99e62298c26439d299606
bbadb00d9439b63cfed42921f767d8316ce42e212082c58a1e5ee1fb619e0fb2f753b0f86
a2db7cace003e5a47efb32a2b4e33d1787d0f6681edfc0737877ee6a28cec242418402cfda
695060bd75f396c909c0b1ba3236519d29291012fbdadd2c8d0d7caae1ea33ac6841b3b6d64ca
69145f7b072304a4f980d907d10b18bee9dd5df8cd8aea6ff11b339e8cc34d7f572c6de69c
53076e8a4f057e46cf6ebe879480f62e1f966abb1f05049b328a3cb47d7208521901e6772
c393251f13ce9ed9daaf21240617a89a813e7c48dbacd099d84979984deecc01e842da38a
199e9e6ef67b84325f18a73c2f9f0fb4c11ce4933eed7728960ad637565e5589dc0faeb84
a28990d71fceb0757f9131e4c151a48df520d427a66c2d2f2d0d4270d4e756c9baa9600da
7f62f8dacf7ab83bb454d5e48e078bad04ade6b98661859c3e9606a5e983a8f7e37d8fac3
b9cc091d518e5b153e8404486533bfc1aa20af4a6633245bc2de2afbf820f9065bae
956690481d0df591dc1073011e6caf8d47f8278f7a0d526a14948c33cc8f252e03c40
d6f91c9a6229770eac49b2498630a468061892420518576dfc0e045598475b68cedb
071e1bf41476569da801081a39e7e658698bb54875ba74ed0af5c95c3fe037b9c8f5f
547c926baa9dd055a4264";
    "IntegratedCircuitCardIdentity" = "89014103211656554643";
    "InternationalMobileSubscriberIdentity" = "310410165655464";
    "InternationalMobileEquipmentIdentity" = "011472002196598";
```

If OpenSSL isn't installed on your desktop, you may also use an online base64 decoding tool, such as the one found at *http://www.opinionatedgeek.com/dot net/tools/Base64Decode/*. Simply paste the encoded portions of the file into the text box and click the Decode button.

## CHAPTER 7

Case Help

Different cases require different types of information. This chapter will cover some of the most common corporate and law enforcement scenarios, and walk through the data you'll want to gather. These scenarios, of course, provide only an overview of the evidence gathering process, so you should be sure to examine all of the evidence, not just what is outlined here.

All of these examples presume that you've already performed forensic recovery of the media partition and can view the live filesystem using one of the tools mentioned in Chapter 5. Some techniques are most easily executed by using the iPhone's user interface, so if you have physical possession of the iPhone, your job will be a little easier.

Employee Suspected of Inappropriate Communication

Inappropriate communication could involve an affair with another coworker, sexual harassment, selling secrets, insider trading, or any other activities that may be a violation of corporate policy. If this is done on a company-owned device, you might have the right to seize the iPhone and conduct an examination.

Live Filesystem

There are many different forms of communication stored on the iPhone, with the two most dominant being email and SMS messages. Other forms of communication might include photos from the user's photo library, which can be attached to outgoing email and online web forms. Finally, the suspect may have made personal notes such as safe combinations or box numbers using the iPhone's notepad, or even have performed map lookups if there was a meeting involved. The following list suggests some key information to check.

SMS messages

Using Chapter 5 as a guide, dump the live SMS database. You'll also want to perform a **strings** dump to recover any deleted messages lurking in unused portions of the file. The SMS database can be found on the iPhone's media partition in */mobile/Library/SMS/sms.db*. Look for both message content and phone numbers.

Email

The second most likely form of communication is email. Scan the Envelope Index located at */mobile/Library/Mail/Envelope Index* for messages in the suspect's inbox as well as in sent mail. This is covered in Chapter 5. A **strings** dump can also be used to recover fragments of communication from deleted messages that may still be lurking in unused portions of the file. If the suspect is using an IMAP mail account, additional messages may be stored on the iPhone in separate files.

 Be careful not to access a suspect's IMAP account online if it requires connecting to a server that is not corporately owned. While locally stored messages on a corporate-owned device might be admissible, it is potentially illegal to access a remote server belonging to the suspect or a third party without a warrant.

Typing cache

The typing cache may contain fragments of past communication, so even if all SMS and email messages have been deleted, you may be able to recover some out-of-context snippets in the cache, which are located at */mobile/Library/Keyboard/dynamic-text.dat*.

 The typing cache is frequently written to by many different applications, so it's important to keep in mind that any fragments you find will be out of context and should be treated as such.

Photo library

If the suspect sent any photos, they may still exist in the photo library on the live filesystem. Check the user's photo library by looking for files in */var/mobile/Media/Photos* and */var/mobile/Media/DCIM*.

Google Maps cache

If the suspect planned any meetings, the Google Maps cache can reveal the addresses or directions that were looked up, and perhaps help to reveal the identities of accomplices or tie the suspect to a victim. For example, if the employee is being investigated for sexual harassment and it has escalated to stalking, you may find directions to the victim's house in the map cache. The Google Maps history can be found at */mobile/Library/Maps/History.plist.*

Voicemail

If the suspect is engaged in two-way communication, check the device for leftover voicemail from others involved. This can be done most easily through the iPhone's user interface, but Chapter 5 guides you through accessing these files from the live filesystem instead. Deleted voicemail can be recovered using data carving, as explained in the next section.

Notes

If the suspect made any notes of events on the device, they can be found in the notes database at */mobile/Library/Notes/notes.db.*

Calendar

To see whether any meetings were scheduled with other people, check the calendar for any events planned. Recovering the calendar is explained in detail in Chapter 5. It is also possible to view live calendar events using the iPhone's user interface.

Call history

If the suspect engaged in any phone calls from the iPhone, a log of those calls should be available through the user interface. A more complete list of calls can be recovered by examining and dumping the call history database at */mobile/Library/CallHistory/call_history.db.*

Data Carving

In addition to the live filesystem, an attempt to recover deleted files from the disk image can be made. Refer to Chapter 4 for instructions on using Scalpel to perform data carving. The following files may aid you in your investigation:

- Deleted images, which may have been used in the communication
- Deleted voicemail, if the suspect engaged in two-way communication with others
- Deleted typing caches, which may reveal older fragments of communication
- Deleted email, which may reveal older correspondence

Strings Dumps

As a last resort, any traces of previous communication can be recovered by performing a `strings` dump of the entire image. You can scan through the output by using a tool like `grep` to zero in on key words. For example, if the suspect is believed to have sent a threat to a coworker named Jane, you can search the entire disk image using the following commands:

```
$ strings rdisk0s2 > strings.txt
$ grep -ni -e jane -e kill -e "going to" strings.txt
```

In this example, a `strings` dump is made and scanned using a case-insensitive search (`-i`) for line numbers (`-n`) and output of text containing any (`-e`) of the following words or phrases: `jane`, `kill`, `going to`. If you find traces of what you are searching for, you can then open the text file and jump to the line containing the text of interest. Surrounding lines of text may include additional communication that may not have appeared in the search.

Employee Destroyed Important Data

On the iPhone, important data can be photos, email, a PDF, or other stored information. Simple information, such as a boarding pass number, can be of great importance if stored somewhere in the browser cache. Data can be destroyed intentionally or by accident, but in either case it's important to understand how to properly recover the lost data. Chapter 4 introduced you to Scalpel, a data-carving tool, which can recover deleted files from a disk image based on the file's header (and optionally, footer). Become intimately familiar with Scalpel, as it is critical for recovering deleted information.

To recover deleted files, Scalpel requires a file header. This represents the first few bytes of the file that can be used to identify the kind of data you're trying to recover. Many examples were given in Chapter 4 to recover some types of proprietary files from the iPhone. Your first attempt at recovering the missing files is to run Scalpel with the rules from Chapter 4.

In the event that some of the data was damaged, it may still be possible to recover pieces of the missing files from the device, especially if they were unstructured communication.

Email
> If part of the message was deleted, you may be able to scan for other parts of the message, such as "Subject: " or a message boundary. Using another message from the same sender, examine the message's source to find the type of message boundary it uses. Some mail agents will use the text NEXTPART followed by a random number, or something similar. Scanning for this with Scalpel will improve your chances of finding the remaining pieces of the message.

Web page data
> If the information was stored on a web page, you may not find it by scanning for <HTML tags, especially if the website didn't use the proper header

tags. Scan for the beginnings of other common tags, such as <META, <BODY, and <SCRIPT. This will increase your chances of recovering fragments of the missing web page.

PDF files and images

Chapter 4 supplied a few different types of PDF and image rules, but not all of these files necessarily share the same headers. Depending on the tool used to generate the PDF or save the image, the format might be slightly different, requiring a different rule. If you know the software package or device used to create the file, create another one and examine it with a hex editor to determine the headers it uses. For example, if you are looking for a very specific image that was taken on a digital camera, use the same camera to take another snapshot, then examine the headers of the new file.

Seized iPhone: Whose Is It and Where Is He?

In some cases, iPhones have been recovered from a crime scene without immediate evidence of whom it belongs to. It could have been dropped by a fleeing suspect or left by a victim. In addition to finding out *who* he is, it may also be important to find out *where* he is. This is especially important if the owner was the victim of a kidnapping or other such crime, or if he is a suspect and possibly dangerous.

Who?

The easiest way to track an iPhone back to its owner is by the phone number. The phone number can be found by tapping on the phone icon, then pressing the Contacts button on the bottom bar. Scroll to the very top of the contacts list and you will see the text My Number, followed by the phone number programmed onto the SIM. This phone number, combined with a subpoena, is usually the easiest way to get a name and address from a telecommunications provider, or possibly from Apple, Inc.[*]

If you are unable to identify the owner based on the phone number, examination of the device can provide you with much more information about the individual:

- Saved email may contain the owner's name and the service provider used. If the owner is connected to his corporate email, you'll be able to find out what company he works for. If a name is unavailable and there are no other useful leads as to the person's identity, consider scanning all email

---

[*] Apple, Inc. is rumored to maintain a database of original iPhone purchasers, tied to the IMEI and/ or serial number of the device.

(including deleted email) for passwords or other account information. If the owner has recently signed up for a new account on any website, there is likely a trail of this somewhere on disk.

- Contact records for people whom the owner frequently communicated with can help lead you to him, especially if he is a victim of a crime. If the owner is a suspect in, say, a murder, you may have just uncovered dozens of new leads.

- The photo library may include photos of the owner, his family, or possible accomplices.

What?

What the owner was doing up to the time of recovering the device may be of particular importance. The following can help determine what kinds of related activities the owner was engaging in:

- Incoming and outgoing SMS text messages will identify people the owner was communicating with, and possibly provide some details about recent activity.

- Stored notes can store details about important information pertaining to the owner.

- Cached web pages can provide hints about what kind of information the owner was interested in. For example, if he is a suspect in a terrorism case, there may be cached pages pertaining to private forums he visited or web searches for explosives.

- The call history can identify individuals with whom the device owner has been in recent contact.

When and Where?

If you are trying to determine the location of the device's owner, the following can provide useful details:

- The Google Maps lookup cache can provide recent lookups of addresses or directions to and from specific addresses. Map tiles can also provide photos of the maps or satellite imagery the owner was recently viewing.

- Calendar entries can identify when and where the owner might be headed in the near future, so that he or his accomplices can be intercepted.

- Clock alarms (normally found by tapping on the Clock application, then tapping the Alarm button) can provide recurring daily or weekly practices, which may help to reveal the individual's location.

- Tapping on the Weather application will allow you to scroll through the cities that the individual is most interested in. Be aware that by default, Cupertino and New York come configured out of the box.
- Tapping on the Maps application should reveal the last area being viewed by the device's owner.

How Can I Be Sure?

If you think you've identified the owner of the device, follow the steps in Chapter 6 to establish a trusted relationship between his iPhone and a desktop machine. This will establish a point of ownership specific to the timestamps of the pairing records.

Disclosures and Source Code

This appendix includes details about the procedures and results described in this book that a court may require from law enforcement witnesses, prosecutors, and defendants.

Power-On Device Modifications (Disclosure)

When any computer is turned on, files are read and written. iPhone examiners need only be concerned with what is written, as the iPhone's filesystem is mounted with the noatime option, even if the option is not specified in /etc/fstab. This option prevents access times from being updated when a file is read or its metadata (such as its name) is changed on the device. Therefore, the access time shown on a file should reflect either its creation or the last time some change was made to the content, allowing you to concentrate on only the files that have been actually changed.

In the likely event that you don't possess special equipment to physically dump the iPhone's memory chip, the device must be powered on and booted into its operating system to recover data. Furthermore, the forensic tools described in this book require that the device be rebooted after the toolkit payload is installed.

Just like a desktop operating system, the iPhone's Leopard operating system performs minor writes to certain files upon booting. The purpose of most writes is to replace or reset existing configuration files, and writes generally don't add any new data to the filesystem. Some writes, however, append a very minor amount of data to files. Overall, the writes to the filesystem are minimal, but are disclosed here in Table A-1 for integrity.

On iPhone firmware versions lower than or equal to 1.1.2, the *mobile* directory is replaced with *root*.

Table A-1. Bytes added to files during boot

Filename	Estimated magnitude of change
/private/var/log/lastlog	28 bytes
/private/var/mobile/Library/Preferences/com.apple.voicemail.plist	1275 bytes
/private/var/preferences/csidata	121 bytes
/private/var/run/configd.pid	3 bytes
/private/var/run/resolv.conf	76 bytes
/private/var/root/Library/Lockdown/data_ark.plist	3252 bytes
/private/var/tmp/MediaCache/diskcacherepository.plist	320 bytes
/private/var/log/wtmp	144 appended
/private/var/mobile/Library/Voicemail/_subscribed	Inode only
/private/var/mobile/Library/Voicemail/voicemail.db	7168 bytes
/private/var/preferences/SystemConfiguration/NetworkInterface.plist	783 bytes
/private/var/preferences/SystemConfiguration/com.apple.AutoWake.plist	730 bytes
/private/var/preferences/SystemConfiguration/com.apple.network.identification.plist	1305 bytes
/private/var/preferences/SystemConfiguration/com.apple.wifi.plist	2284 bytes
/private/var/preferences/SystemConfiguration/preferences.plist	4380 bytes

Unless otherwise noted, all changes are performed as overwrites to existing data, but this isn't guaranteed.

In addition to the changes noted in Table A-1, the files listed in Table A-2 may be written to or recreated when someone logs into the device, causing bytes to be added.

Table A-2. Bytes added to files during login

Filename	Estimated magnitude of change
/private/var/run/utmp	468 bytes
/private/var/run/utmpx	1256 bytes

Installation Record (Disclosure)

The forensic toolkit payload installed by iLiberty+ places a set of open source tools onto the otherwise read-only portion of the device, resulting in no destruction to user-level data stored on the device's media partition. At the time of payload installation, the following files are written to the system (root) partition.

 File size may vary depending on the application and payload versions used. Some files are deleted after toolkit installation.

```
/usr/libexec/ipluspwns (basepack)
-rwxr-xr-x  1 root wheel     25212 Mar 27 08:59 chmod*
-rwxr-xr-x  1 root wheel     38320 Mar 27 08:59 echo*
-rwxr-xr-x  1 root wheel     23292 Mar 27 08:59 iPipe*
-rwxr-xr-x  1 root wheel     14352 Mar 27 08:59 mv*
-rwxr-xr-x  1 root wheel     13760 Mar 27 08:59 reboot*
-rwxr-xr-x  1 root wheel     19128 Mar 27 08:59 rm*
-rwxr-xr-x  1 root wheel   1298880 Mar 27 08:59 sh*
-rwxr-xr-x  1 root wheel     39036 Mar 27 08:59 sleep*
-rwxr-xr-x  1 root wheel     14916 Mar 27 08:59 umount*
-rwxr-xr-x  1 root wheel    141528 Mar 27 08:59 unzip*
        /bin (basepack)
-rwxr-xr-x  1 root  wheel    134152 Mar 27 08:59 awk
-rwxr-xr-x  1 root  wheel     23368 Mar 27 08:59 blcheck
-rwxr-xr-x  1 root  wheel     14368 Mar 27 08:59 cat
-rwxr-xr-x  1 root  wheel     25212 Mar 27 08:59 chmod
-rwxr-xr-x  1 root  wheel     80660 Mar 27 08:59 chown
-rwxr-xr-x  1 root  wheel     19644 Mar 27 08:59 cp
-rwxr-xr-x  1 root  wheel     18972 Mar 27 08:59 cut
-rwxr-xr-x  1 root  wheel     33288 Mar 27 08:59 dd
-rwxr-xr-x  1 root  wheel      9212 Mar 27 08:59 dirname
-rw-r--r--  1 root  wheel      2971 Apr  1 20:25 functions.inc
-rwxr-xr-x  1 root  wheel    158708 Mar 27 08:59 grep
-rwxr-xr-x  1 root  wheel     18056 Mar 31 14:03 iEdit
-rwxr-xr-x  1 root  wheel     20776 Mar 27 08:59 igsm
-rwxr-xr-x  1 root  wheel     13492 Mar 31 14:03 ln
-rwxr-xr-x  1 root  wheel     41028 Mar 27 08:59 ls
-rwxr-xr-x  1 root  wheel     13348 Mar 31 14:03 mkdir
-rwxr-xr-x  1 root  wheel     24244 Mar 27 08:59 plutil
-rwxr-xr-x  1 root  wheel     13760 Mar 27 08:59 reboot
-rwxr-xr-x  1 root  wheel     19172 Mar 27 08:59 rm
-rwxr-xr-x  1 root  wheel     42888 Mar 27 08:59 sed
-rwxr-xr-x  1 root  wheel   1298880 Mar 27 08:59 sh
-rwxr-xr-x  1 root  wheel      9392 Mar 27 08:59 sleep
-rwxr-xr-x  1 root  wheel    260244 Mar 27 08:59 tar
-rwxr-xr-x  1 root  wheel    141528 Mar 27 08:59 unzip
        /bin (payload)
```

```
-rwxr-xr-x  1 root  wheel   591364 Mar 16 09:23 bash
-rwxr-xr-x  1 root  wheel    45804 Feb 29 04:55 cat
-rwxr-xr-x  1 root  wheel    74456 Feb 29 04:55 chgrp
-rwxr-xr-x  1 root  wheel    65632 Feb 29 04:55 chmod
-rwxr-xr-x  1 root  wheel    74724 Feb 29 04:55 chown
-rwxr-xr-x  1 root  wheel   159704 Feb 29 04:55 cp
-rwxr-xr-x  1 root  wheel    33288 Apr  7 10:25 dd
-rwxr-xr-x  1 root  wheel   119948 Mar 27 07:48 grep
-rwxr-xr-x  1 root  wheel   115848 Feb 29 04:55 ln
-rwxr-xr-x  1 root  wheel   146360 Feb 29 04:55 ls
-rwxr-xr-x  1 root  wheel    44452 Feb 29 04:55 mkdir
-rwxr-xr-x  1 root  wheel    45900 Feb 29 04:55 mknod
-rwxr-xr-x  1 root  wheel   169368 Feb 29 04:55 mv
-rwxr-xr-x  1 root  wheel    39292 Feb 29 04:55 pwd
-rwxr-xr-x  1 root  wheel    13760 Apr  8 00:35 reboot
-rwxr-xr-x  1 root  wheel   142636 Feb 29 04:55 rm
lrwxr-xr-x  1 root  wheel        4 Apr  8 00:18 sh -> bash
-rwxr-xr-x  1 root  wheel    17004 Feb 27 18:50 sync
     /etc (payload)
-rw-r--r--  1 root  wheel     1418 Jun 12  2006 ssh_config
-rw-r--r--  1 root  wheel     3230 Aug 25  2007 sshd_config
     /sbin (payload)
-rwxr-xr-x  1 root  wheel   185008 Apr  8 00:34 fsck_hfs
-rwxr-xr-x  1 root  wheel    18052 May  7 12:12 md5
-rwxr-xr-x  1 root  wheel    19236 Apr  8 00:34 mount_hfs
-rwxr-xr-x  1 root  wheel    46300 Apr  8 00:35 newfs_hfs
-rwxr-xr-x  1 root  wheel   191976 May  7 12:22 ping
-rwxr-xr-x  1 root  wheel    14916 Apr  8 00:37 umount
     /usr/bin (payload)
-rwsr-xr-x  1 root  wheel    31712 Feb 27 18:50 login
-rwxr-xr-x  1 root  wheel    29520 Apr  8 00:34 nc
-rwxr-xr-x  1 root  wheel    56284 Aug 23  2007 scp
-rwxr-xr-x  1 root  wheel    88876 Aug 23  2007 sftp
-rwxr-xr-x  1 root  wheel   340340 Aug 23  2007 ssh
-rwxr-xr-x  1 root  wheel   103960 Aug 23  2007 ssh-add
-rwxr-xr-x  1 root  wheel    87336 Aug 23  2007 ssh-agent
-rwxr-xr-x  1 root  wheel   134264 Aug 23  2007 ssh-keygen
-rwxr-xr-x  1 root  wheel   198048 Aug 23  2007 ssh-keyscan


     /usr/lib (payload)
lrwxr-xr-x  1 root  wheel       18 Apr  8 00:18 libcurses.dylib ->
                                                libncurses.5.dylib
-r-xr-xr-x  1 root  wheel    35392 Jan  3 20:31 libhistory.5.2.dylib
lrwxr-xr-x  1 root  wheel       20 Apr  8 00:18 libhistory.5.dylib ->
                                                libhistory.5.2.dylib
lrwxr-xr-x  1 root  wheel       20 Apr  8 00:18 libhistory.dylib ->
                                                libhistory.5.2.dylib
-rw-r--r--  1 root  wheel    60780 Jan 14 21:44 libintl.8.0.2.dylib
lrwxr-xr-x  1 root  wheel       19 Apr  8 00:18 libintl.8.dylib ->
                                                libintl.8.0.2.dylib
lrwxr-xr-x  1 root  wheel       19 Apr  8 00:18 libintl.dylib ->
                                                libintl.8.0.2.dylib
-rw-r--r--  1 root  wheel      801 Jan 14 21:44 libintl.la
```

```
-rwxr-xr-x  1 root  wheel  105156 Feb 23 06:30 libncurses++.a
-rwxr-xr-x  1 root  wheel  379360 Feb 23 06:30 libncurses.5.dylib
lrwxr-xr-x  1 root  wheel      18 Apr  8 00:18 libncurses.dylib ->
                                              libncurses.5.dylib
-r-xr-xr-x  1 root  wheel  239308 Jan  3 20:31 libreadline.5.2.dylib
lrwxr-xr-x  1 root  wheel      21 Apr  8 00:18 libreadline.5.dylib ->
                                              libreadline.5.2.dylib
lrwxr-xr-x  1 root  wheel      21 Apr  8 00:18 libreadline.dylib ->
                                              libreadline.5.2.dylib
-rwxr-xr-x  1 root  wheel  247684 Jan  4 05:35 libresolv.dylib
lrwxr-xr-x  1 root  wheel      17 Apr  8 00:18 terminfo -> ../share/terminfo


      /usr/libexec (payload)
-rwxr-xr-x  1 root  wheel   59372 Aug 23  2007 sftp-server
-rwxr-xr-x  1 root  wheel  200664 Aug 23  2007 ssh-keysign
-rwxr-xr-x  1 root  wheel   35280 Aug 23  2007 ssh-rand-helper
-r-xr-xr-x  1 root  wheel     425 Dec 20  2006 sshd-keygen-wrapper

      /usr/sbin (payload)
-rwxr-xr-x  1 root  wheel   32784 Apr  8 00:36 fdisk
-rwxr-xr-x  1 root  wheel  414512 Aug 23  2007 sshd

      /Library/LaunchDaemons (payload)
-rw-r--r--  1 root  wheel     828 Feb  4  2006 com.openssh.sshd.plist
```

Technical Procedure

This section explains some low-level technical details of the operations performed by the iLiberty+ tool. These techniques are intended for those desiring a technical explanation of the procedure or who seek to reproduce or reimplement it, and are not necessary for general forensic examination.

Many different methods have been devised by the iPhone development community to gain access to an iPhone's operating system, but very few of them are able to do so without destroying evidence, or even destroying the entire filesystem. The technique used in this manual is considered to be forensically safe in that it is capable of accessing the device without corrupting user data.

Unsigned RAM Disks

A RAM disk is a filesystem that resides in memory, and is not physically written on disk. Most Unix kernels are capable of booting the operating system from memory, and most versions of iPhone software also support this.

The technique used by iLiberty+ for iPhone software versions 1.0.2–1.1.4 gains access to the operating system by booting an unsigned RAM disk from the iPhone's resident memory. This RAM disk is copied into the iPhone's memory and booted by setting the appropriate kernel flags using Apple's Mobile-Device framework. This section is based specifically on version 7.4.2 of the device framework. Because the function calls change slightly for newer versions of the framework, you will have to install this framework with a copy of iTunes 7.4.2 in order to reproduce the procedure in this section.

Once the unsigned RAM disk is booted, the iPhone's disk-based filesystem is mounted and the selected payload is copied. Depending on the payload, this could simply enable shell access, or install a surveillance kit or any other type of software. When the device boots back into its normal operating mode, the installed payload will be executed, performing whatever tasks it was designed for.

iLiberty+'s custom RAM disk differs from the RAM disk used by Apple to install software updates and perform restores. The custom iLiberty+ RAM disk consists of a disk image containing the necessary ARM-architecture files to boot and install a custom payload on the iPhone. The RAM disk itself is padded with 0x800 bytes to contain an 8900 header, and may additionally pad between 0xCC2000 and 0xD1000 zero bytes to assist in aligning the execution space of the disk.

Once a custom RAM disk has been assembled, it is executed using private and undocumented function calls within Apple's MobileDevice framework. In short, this involves the following procedures.

The device is placed into recovery mode either manually (by holding the Home and Power buttons until forced into recovery mode), or by using the Mobile-Device function AMDeviceEnterRecovery. The RAM disk image is sent to the device using the private __sendFileToDevice function after looking up its symbol address in the framework.

The following commands are sent to the device using the private __sendCommandToDevice function after looking up its symbol address in the MobileDevice framework. This sets the kernel's boot arguments to boot from a RAM disk, and specifies the memory address of the approximate location of the custom image copied to the device.

```
setenv boot-args rd=md0 -s -x pmd0=0x9340000.0xA00000
saveenv
fsboot
```

Depending on the capacity and firmware version of the device, different memory addresses may be necessary. The memory address 0x09CC2000.0x0133D000 has also been reported to succeed.

Once the RAM disk has booted and the payload has been delivered, the device can be booted back into normal operating mode by sending the following commands to the device using __sendCommandToDevice:

```
setenv boot-args [Empty]
setenv auto-boot true
saveenv
fsboot
```

 Depending on the version of iPhone firmware, the fsboot command may be replaced with bootx.

Source Code Examples

The following source code illustrates the process of booting an unsigned RAM disk in C. The example waits for the device to be connected in recovery mode and then issues the commands to send and boot a RAM disk as described in the previous section. The RAM disk image and needed framework library are provided by the implementer. This code was designed to run on the Mac OS X operating system running iTunes 7.4.2 MobileDevice framework. Comments are provided inline.

To build this example, use the following command:

```
$ gcc -o inject-ramdisk inject-ramdisk.c -framework CoreFoundation
-framework MobileDevice -F/System/Library/PrivateFrameworks
```

The complete code for inject-ramdisk.c follows:

```c
#include <stdio.h>
#include <mach-o/nlist.h>
#include <CoreFoundation/CoreFoundation.h>

/* Path to the MobileDevice framework is used to look up symbols and
offsets */
#define MOBILEDEVICE_FRAMEWORK
"/System/Library/PrivateFrameworks/MobileDevice.framework/Versions/A/
MobileDevice"

/* Used as a pointer to the iPhone/iTouch device, when booted into
recovery */
typedef struct AMRecoveryModeDevice *AMRecoveryModeDevice_t;

/* Memory pointers to private functions inside the MobileDevice framework */
typedef int(*symbol) (AMRecoveryModeDevice_t, CFStringRef) \
    __attribute__ ((regparm(2)));
static symbol sendCommandToDevice;
static symbol sendFileToDevice;
```

```c
/* Very simple symbol lookup. Returns the position of the function in
memory */
static unsigned int loadSymbol (const char *path, const char *name)
{
    struct nlist nl[2];
    memset(&nl, 0, sizeof(nl));
    nl[0].n_un.n_name = (char *) name;
    if (nlist(path, nl) < 0 || nl[0].n_type == N_UNDF) {
        return 0;
    }
    return nl[0].n_value;
}


/* How to proceed when the device is connected in recovery mode.
* This is the function responsible for sending the ramdisk image and booting
* into the memory location containing it. */

void Recovery_Connect(AMRecoveryModeDevice_t device) {
    int r;

    fprintf(stderr, "Recovery_Connect: DEVICE CONNECTED in Recovery Mode\n");

    /* Upload RAM disk image from file */
    r = sendFileToDevice(device, CFSTR("ramdisk.bin"));
    fprintf(stderr, "sendFileToDevice returned %d\n", r);

    /* Set the boot environment arguments sent to the kernel */
    r = sendCommandToDevice(device,
        CFSTR("setenv boot-args rd=md0 -s -x pmd0=0x9340000.0xA00000"));
    fprintf(stderr, "sendCommandToDevice returned %d\n", r);

    /* Instruct the device to save the environment variable change */
    r = sendCommandToDevice(device, CFSTR("saveenv"));
    fprintf(stderr, "sendCommandToDevice returned %d\n", r);

    /* Invoke boot sequence (bootx may also be used) */
    r = sendCommandToDevice(device, CFSTR("fsboot"));
    fprintf(stderr, "sendCommandToDevice returned %d\n", r);
}

/* Used for notification only */
void Recovery_Disconnect(AMRecoveryModeDevice_t device) {

    fprintf(stderr, "Recovery_Disconnect: Device Disconnected\n");
}

/* Main program loop */
int main(int argc, char *argv[]) {
    AMRecoveryModeDevice_t recoveryModeDevice;
    unsigned int r;

    /* Find the __sendCommandToDevice and __sendFileToDevice symbols */
    sendCommandToDevice = (symbol) loadSymbol
        (MOBILEDEVICE_FRAMEWORK, "__sendCommandToDevice");
```

```
if (!sendCommandToDevice) {
    fprintf(stderr, "ERROR: Could not locate symbol: "
        "__sendCommandToDevice in %s\n", MOBILEDEVICE_FRAMEWORK);
    return EXIT_FAILURE;
}
fprintf(stderr, "sendCommandToDevice: %08x\n", sendCommandToDevice);

sendFileToDevice = (symbol) loadSymbol
    (MOBILEDEVICE_FRAMEWORK, "__sendFileToDevice");
if (!sendFileToDevice) {
    fprintf(stderr, "ERROR: Could not locate symbol: "
        "__sendFileToDevice in %s\n", MOBILEDEVICE_FRAMEWORK);
    return EXIT_FAILURE;
}

/* Invoke callback functions for recovery mode connect and disconnect */
r = AMRestoreRegisterForDeviceNotifications(
    NULL,
    Recovery_Connect,
    NULL,
    Recovery_Disconnect,
    0,
    NULL);
fprintf(stderr, "AMRestoreRegisterForDeviceNotifications returned %d\n",
r);
fprintf(stderr, "Waiting for device in restore mode...\n");

/* Loop */
CFRunLoopRun();
}
```

Once the RAM disk has been injected and booted, iLiberty+'s work is complete and the RAM disk has delivered whatever payload it was written to deliver. The device can then be returned to normal operating mode by issuing the following commands in place of those in the Recovery_Connect function:

```
/* Reset and save the default boot-related environment variables */
sendCommandToDevice(device, CFSTR("setenv auto-boot true"));
sendCommandToDevice(device, CFSTR("setenv boot-args "));
sendCommandToDevice(device, CFSTR("saveenv"));

/* Boot the device (bootx may also be used) */
sendCommandToDevice(device, CFSTR("fsboot"));
```

The device will now boot into normal operating mode for all subsequent boots.

Index

We'd like to hear your suggestions for improving our indexes. Send email to *index@oreilly.com*.

About the Author

Jonathan Zdziarski is better known as the hacker "NerveGas" in the iPhone development community. His work in cracking the iPhone and helped lead the effort to port the first open source applications. Hailed on many geek news sites for his accomplishments, Jonathan is best known for the first application to illustrate and take full advantage of the major iPhone APIs: NES.app, a portable Nintendo Entertainment System emulator.

Jonathan is also a full-time research scientist and longtime spam fighter. He is founder of the DSPAM project, a high-profile, next-generation spam filter that was acquired in 2006 by a company designing software accelerators. He lectures widely on the topic of spam and is a foremost researcher in the fields of machine-learning and algorithmic theory.

Colophon

Our look is the result of reader comments, our own experimentation, and feedback from distribution channels. Distinctive covers complement our distinctive approach to technical topics, breathing personality and life into potentially dry subjects.

The animals on the cover of *iPhone Forensics* are least weasels (*Mustela nivalis*). There are 67 species of weasel, including the mink, ermine, ferret, otter, and skunk. Weasels, who are characterized by long, slender bodies and short legs, are found on all continents except Antarctica and Australia, and in a vast variety of habitats. The least weasel is the smallest of the 67 species of weasel. Weighing in at approximately two ounces and measuring less than ten inches long, the least weasel is the smallest carnivore on Earth. They are found throughout the world, in northern climates. In warm weather this weasel's coat is brown, with a white underside. In winter it turns completely white. Thanks to its camouflage abilities and its speed and agility, the least weasel is rarely caught.

The diet of the least weasel is made up primarily of voles and mice, which, because of the weasels' high metabolism, they hunt constantly. One family of these little weasels can consume thousands of rodents each year, making them important in controlling pest populations. Because it is so small, the least weasel can follow mice into their burrows and eat them there. Like other weasels, they will occasionally then make their victim's home their own, lining it with the fur of the former resident when preparing to nest. Least weasels can produce two litters a year, with three to five young per litter.

The cover image is from *Lydekker's Library of Natural History*. The cover font is Adobe ITC Garamond. The text font is Linotype Birka; the heading font is Adobe Myriad Condensed; and the code font is LucasFont's TheSansMono-Condensed.

Related Titles from O'Reilly

Security

802.11 Security

Apache Security

Building Internet Firewalls, *2nd Edition*

Computer Security Basics, *2nd Edition*

Digital Identity

Hardening Cisco Routers

Internet Forensics

Kerberos: The Definitive Guide

Linux Security Cookbook

Managing Security with Snort and IDS Tools

Mastering FreeBSD OpenBSD Security

Network Security Assessment , *2nd Edition*

Network Security Hacks, *2nd Edition*

Network Security with OpenSSL

Network Security Tools

Network Warrior

Practical Unix and Internet Security, *3rd Edition*

Programming .NET Security

RADIUS

Secure Coding: Principles and Practices

Secure Programming Cookbook for C and C++

Security and Usability

Security Power Tools

Security Warrior

SSH, The Secure Shell: The Definitive Guide, *2nd Edition*

Snort Cookbook

SpamAssassin

Web Security, Privacy and Commerce, *2nd Edition*

Windows Server 2003 Security Cookbook

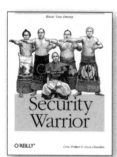

O'REILLY®

Our books are available at most retail and online bookstores.

To order direct: 1-800-998-9938 • *order@oreilly.com* • *www.oreilly.com*

Online editions of most O'Reilly titles are available by subscription at *safari.oreilly.com*